CW01657807

LEADING BY DESIGN

THE LEADERSHIP SECRET NO ONE TELLS YOU

Written By

ROBERT LEE BARBER

Copyright © 2024 Paratus Consulting LLC.
All rights reserved.

No part of this book may be reproduced, distributed, or transmitted in any form or by any means, including photocopying, recording, or other electronic or mechanical methods, without the prior written permission of the publisher, except in the case of brief quotations embodied in critical reviews and certain other noncommercial uses permitted by copyright law. For permission requests, write to the publisher, addressed "Attention: Permissions Coordinator," at the address below:

Paratus Consulting LLC - 1100 Market Street
Chattanooga, TN 37419

Disclaimer:

The information in this book is intended for educational and informational purposes only. Paratus Consulting LLC makes no representations or warranties with respect to the accuracy, applicability, fitness, or completeness of the contents of this book. This book has been edited with the assistance of AI technology, specifically ChatGPT. While the author has created, curated, and refined all content, AI tools were utilized to enhance clarity, structure, and expression throughout the manuscript. The insights and opinions presented are those of the author. We disclaim any warranties (expressed or implied). Paratus Consulting LLC shall in no event be held liable for any loss or other damages, including but not limited to special, incidental, consequential, or other damages.

CONTENTS

ACKNOWLEDGEMENTS

My first introduction to formal leadership came in high school JROTC, where I learned about the hierarchy of leadership. But it wasn't until I attended Valley Forge Military College that I encountered what leadership truly looked like—both the inspiring and the deeply flawed. At just 17, I found myself thrust into a world that was equal parts structured discipline and chaotic extremes. It was a unique environment: some students were there because their parents saw it as a last resort, while others were active-duty service members, 22 to 25 years old, striving to earn a coveted spot at a prestigious military academy.

In that crucible of personalities and experiences, I witnessed leadership at its best—and its worst. Yet, one individual stood out and forever shaped my understanding of what it means to lead. He was a Sergeant Major at the school, an already accomplished Army Ranger aspiring to become an officer. Though he held a senior position, he embodied both the structure and humanity of leadership in a way that left an indelible mark on me.

I'll never forget my first drill weekend. A Florida boy suddenly thrust into the freezing Northeast winter, I made a rookie mistake: I forgot my heavy drill jacket. As we stood in formation for a gear check, I was called out and thoroughly reprimanded in front of the entire platoon. It was harsh and humiliating. But what happened next was something I'll carry with me forever.

After the dressing down, the Sergeant Major pulled me aside. He didn't just explain why I had been reprimanded; he taught me why it mattered. He emphasized the importance of being prepared, shared a personal story of his own mistakes, and then did something I never expected—he handed me his own heavy jacket for the week. Throughout those cold, grueling days, wearing his jacket with his name and rank stitched on it, I learned my first true lesson in leadership: accountability matters, but so does having someone's back.

That moment hooked me. It sparked a lifelong curiosity about leadership—not just as a position of authority but as a practice that blends discipline and humanity. Over the years, I've been privileged to lead in many different capacities, each one deepening my understanding of what it means to guide and support others. Along the way, I discovered that leadership is actually a process that can be taught.

What I learned in those early military days—and later while leading in Fortune 150 environments and as an entrepreneur—is what this book seeks to share. Leadership is not just theory; it is a process. It's about structure and execution, but it's also deeply personal. It requires a clear framework, but it must always remain human.

As I reflect on this journey, I want to acknowledge and thank Sergeant Major S (Anonymous), Valley Forge Military College, Class of 1989. That lesson, the leadership he exhibited, and the humanity he demonstrated have stayed with me and planted the seed for this book so many years later.

This book is not about how to lead like the military or choosing between structure and humanity; it's about using structure as a tool to amplify your humanity as a leader. It's about understanding that leadership is a process, not just an abstract concept, and that process enables you to bring your authentic self to the role. By embracing both, you can build environments where people feel both grounded and empowered, where clarity fosters creativity, and where discipline enables compassion.

Leadership that combines process and humanity doesn't just drive results—it transforms teams, organizations, and individuals.

PREFACE

Welcome to The Leadership Secret No One Tells You

Leadership: It is Actually A Process.

Have you ever worked under a bad leader? The kind that made every day feel like an absolute nightmare, where decisions were chaotic, and direction was nonexistent? The kind of leader that made your Sunday night so dreadful with the anticipation of being in their Monday morning meeting? Or maybe you've had the privilege of following a great leader—someone whose clarity and consistency inspired you to give your best every single day. Leadership is one of those things you recognize most when it's absent—like gravity. Without it to hold everything in place, chaos ensues. But what if I told you there's more to great leadership than just charisma or intuition?

Early in my career, I stumbled into this truth. By sheer luck, my first job as an engineer landed me at the first foreign company to win the Deming Prize. At the time, I didn't realize just how significant that was. The Deming Prize, named after W. Edwards Deming, is one of the most prestigious awards in the world of business. It recognizes organizations that exemplify excellence in quality and process management.

The story behind the Deming Prize is as fascinating as the man himself. After World War II, Japan faced the daunting task of rebuilding its shattered economy and re-establishing its industries. General Douglas MacArthur, overseeing the Allied occupation of Japan, understood that a stable and prosperous Japan was essential for long-term peace in the region. To support this effort, Japanese leaders sought international expertise to transform their manufacturing sector into a global competitor.

W. Edwards Deming, already a respected figure in statistical quality control, was invited to Japan in 1950 by the Union of Japanese Scientists and Engineers (JUSE). While his work had been underutilized in the United States, Deming's focus on process improvement and statistical methods aligned perfectly with Japan's need for economic recovery. He taught Japanese engineers and executives the principles of quality management, emphasizing the importance of continuous improvement, statistical control of processes, and fostering a culture of innovation and accountability.

Deming's methods were not just theoretical—they were transformative. His teachings sparked a manufacturing revolution in Japan, positioning the country as a leader in industries like automobiles and electronics. Companies like Toyota and Sony became synonymous with precision, quality, and reliability, thanks to Deming's philosophies. The Deming Prize was established in his honor, cementing his legacy as a key architect of Japan's post-war resurgence.

Winning the Deming Prize is more than a recognition of success; it is a testament to an organization's mastery of process-driven excellence—a principle that continues to guide the most successful businesses worldwide.

For me, this wasn't just an introduction to Deming's principles; it was an indoctrination. I quickly learned that a business is, at its core, a bundle of processes assigned to talented people. Those who can better define their processes—and assign the best talent to execute them—win. This simple yet profound realization became my leadership north star and a philosophy I would carry into every role I held thereafter.

Years later, as an HR executive overseeing acquisitions across the country, I saw this principle come to life in an entirely new way. Each plant we acquired had its own culture, shaped by the habits and traditions of its workforce. But as we installed our processes, something remarkable happened. Over time, those processes began to imprint our DNA onto these sites.

At first, there would be resistance. People pushed back, clinging to the ways they had always done things. But processes don't just create efficiency—they create consistency. And consistency, applied persistently, shapes behaviors, forges habits, and ultimately defines culture. Slowly but surely, our processes became the backbone of these plants. They began to look less like their old selves and more like us—not because we demanded it, but because our processes naturally led them there.

It was during this time that I also saw a surprising truth: many of the top companies we encountered lacked robust processes altogether. They relied on talent, luck, and a patchwork of habits rather than the deliberate systems Deming championed. Those businesses struggled to scale, adapt, and thrive in the face of challenges because their foundations were built on sand, not stone.

These experiences solidified my belief: process isn't just a management tool; it's the essence of leadership. By defining, refining, and executing processes, leaders create the frameworks that allow talent to thrive and cultures to flourish. This book is a culmination of that journey—a guide to understanding leadership not as an abstract art but as a practical science, rooted in the deliberate design and execution of process.

Leadership is often perceived as an abstract quality, yet it is far more concrete and systemic than many realize. It can be likened to a mathematical equation where process creates behaviors, consistent behaviors establish habits, and habits ultimately forge the culture of an organization. Leadership, therefore, is the mastery of developing these processes that in turn cultivate a thriving culture. This approach demystifies leadership, showing it not as something ethereal and nebulous, but as a skill rooted in the creation and reinforcement of productive habits.

I firmly believe that leadership is not an innate gift reserved for a select few but a skill that can be learned, practiced, and mastered. Great leaders aren't born—they're built through deliberate effort, reflection, and the application of proven principles. Leadership is a process, not a mystery, and anyone willing to engage in that process can become extraordinary. I often say - "In God I trust—and in leaders who trust the process."

Often, we complicate leadership more than necessary, obscuring its essence behind a veil of jargon and abstract theory. However, at its core, leadership is far more systematic and tangible than many might suggest. It's not solely a personal style or an inherent trait; it's a process—a repeatable and measurable method to achieve specific outcomes.

The misconception that leadership must be a complex, elusive skill can deter potential leaders from embracing their capabilities. In reality, leadership is like any other skill that can be learned, practiced, and mastered. This book aims to strip away the complexities typically associated with leadership and return to the basics—transforming it from an art only a few can practice to a science that many can learn and implement.

In the modern professional landscape, we encounter a myriad array of leadership models and theories. While these can be valuable, they sometimes add layers of complexity that are unnecessary. The heart of effective leadership lies in its simplicity. By understanding leadership as a process, leaders can develop clear strategies that are easy to communicate and implement, ensuring that their actions lead to predictable and positive outcomes.

Our approach in this book, which emphasizes process over persona, is about crafting behaviors, reinforcing habits, and ultimately building a culture. As leaders, our primary role is not to do the work ourselves or to provide all the answers. Instead, it is to create the environment and furnish the resources that enable our teams to journey through their tasks and challenges. This framework is foundational to understanding leadership as a process—a systematic approach that cultivates the right behaviors, habits, and ultimately, a thriving culture that drives performance. When we step in to solve every problem or answer every query, we inadvertently rob our team members of their individual growth and the opportunity to develop their problem-solving capabilities.

Consider this: every great director knows that their job is to enable the actors to give their best performance; the director never steps into the role of the actor themselves. Similarly, effective leaders understand that their responsibility is to guide their teams towards autonomy and success. This means creating an environment where team members feel supported yet challenged, equipped yet compelled to stretch their abilities. A leader's first job from 50,000 ft is to foster the culture.

Trait Theory vs. Process Theory

Before we go any further, let's get a little academic. Let's talk about trait theory vs. process theory leadership. Yes, this is a thing.

Let's do a quick 101 together—I needed this along the way in my pursuit of excellence in leadership just as much as you do now on this journey. I knew this process approach worked, but I didn't have the language to describe what I witnessed in real life: leadership that could be taught, repeated, and scaled.

Trait theory posits that leadership is rooted in innate qualities—characteristics that some individuals are simply born with. Traits like charisma, confidence, decisiveness, and intelligence are thought to separate leaders from followers. It's an appealing idea: the notion that leadership is a natural gift, tied to who you are rather than what you do.

Process theory, on the other hand, flips the script. It asserts that leadership is a set of behaviors and actions that anyone can learn and master. Leadership isn't a fixed quality; it's a skill. It's not about innate traits but about how you engage, communicate, and execute in a consistent and deliberate way.

Here's the reality: traits matter, but they're not enough or even the start. Charisma might draw people in, but it won't sustain momentum. Confidence can inspire trust, but it won't achieve results on its own. That's why process theory—and frameworks like **Leading By Design**—matter so much.

Leading By Design provides a clear, structured process approach to leadership, emphasizing repeatable processes that drive results and create alignment. It's where leaders should start—not because trait theory is irrelevant, but because process gives leadership a foundation. With a process-first mindset, leaders can intentionally cultivate their strengths, develop their teams, and deliver consistent outcomes.

Traits can amplify your leadership, but **process is the foundation that makes it sustainable and scalable.** You can't control your natural traits, but you can control your actions. That's why Leading By Design is essential—it turns leadership into something tangible, measurable, and teachable.

The bottom line? Leadership isn't just about what you have or are born with—it's about what you build. Start with process. Traits may enhance your effectiveness, but a strong foundation in process ensures you have the structure and tools to lead with purpose and achieve meaningful results.

Why A Process?

As an engineer, I've always appreciated the elegance of breaking complex problems into simple, solvable equations. Leadership, at its core, is no different. While it might seem like a complex web of decisions, emotions, and interactions, it can be distilled into a straightforward formula that anyone can follow. At the heart of this formula is a deliberate process—a repeatable, logical sequence that transforms intentions into results.

The environment leaders create doesn't happen overnight, nor does it come about by chance. It is the outcome of a process—a carefully designed and executed system. This process initiates a chain reaction:

PROCESS creates **BEHAVIORS**,
BEHAVIORS creates **HABITS**,
HABITS creates **CULTURE**,
CULTURE creates **PERFORMANCE**

Think of it as the leadership equivalent of a mathematical chain reaction, where each step compounds upon the last:

1. Processes establish the framework and structure for how things are done.
2. These processes influence behaviors, shaping how people act and interact.
3. Repeated behaviors solidify into habits, which become automatic and enduring.
4. Collectively, these habits define the culture, the underlying essence of how a team or organization operates.
5. A strong, aligned culture drives performance, achieving results consistently and predictably.

The beauty of this chain reaction is its simplicity. You don't need to be a charismatic visionary or a natural-born leader to succeed—you need clarity and consistency in executing processes that drive the right outcomes. Leadership is less about innate ability and more about embracing the logic of this chain reaction and committing to its application.

When you focus on refining the process, the rest of the chain reaction falls into place. The process dictates behaviors, which shape habits, which create the culture that powers performance. Leadership, then, is not an art reserved for a select few but a science available to anyone willing to put in the effort to learn and execute this straightforward math.

This chain reaction is more than a metaphor; it's a practical guide for leaders at every level. By understanding and applying this, you can design and implement systems that produce consistent results, build a thriving culture, and lead your team to unparalleled performance—all with the simplicity and clarity of basic math. Lets take this chain reaction and design a formula we can apply to our leadership.

Lets call it **The Leadership Algorithm**.

$$P + B^2 + H^3 = C^4 \rightarrow \text{Perf}$$

In the context of leadership, an "algorithm" can be understood as a set of predefined, systematic instructions or processes designed to achieve specific outcomes within an organization. When referring to the Leading By Design leadership chain reaction —**PROCESS creates BEHAVIORS, BEHAVIORS create HABITS, HABITS create CULTURE, CULTURE creates PERFORMANCE**—the term "algorithm" emphasizes the methodical and predictable nature of how these elements interact and lead to desired results.

Let's break The Leadership Algorithm down:

P (Process): This is the starting point. Effective processes are the foundation upon which behaviors are built. They set the stage for how tasks are approached and managed within the team.

B^2 (Behaviors Squared): The square symbolizes that behaviors are reinforced over time through continuous practice and feedback. These are the direct outcomes of robust processes, and when repeated, they strengthen and become more ingrained.

H^3 (Habits Cubed): Cubing represents the exponential impact of habits. Habits are behaviors that have become automatic through repetition. The cube emphasizes how ingrained habits become powerful drivers within the team, affecting actions without conscious thought.

C^4 (Culture to the Fourth Power): The fourth power indicates the profound influence of culture. It is a multiplier of all the habits established within a group, permeating every aspect of organizational life and magnifying the effects of the foundational habits.

Perf (Leads to Performance): The arrow signifies the outcome or result of the equation. When process, behaviors, habits, and culture are aligned, they lead directly to enhanced performance. This represents not just the achievement of goals but the maximization of the team's potential.

This leadership algorithm not only captures the logical flow from processes to performance but also highlights the compounding effect of each component. It's a simple yet powerful way to communicate the importance of foundational elements in achieving high performance, making it clear that robust processes and consistent behaviors are vital to cultivating a strong culture and outstanding performance.

For instance, by consistently providing teams with the tools and training they need to solve problems, leaders foster a behavior of self-sufficiency. Over time, this behavior becomes a habit, ingrained in the team's daily routines and mindset. Ultimately, it shapes a culture of independence and confidence, crucial elements that drive organizational performance.

In this equation, each component is vital. The process must be thoughtfully designed to encourage the right behaviors—those that align with the organization's goals and values. When these behaviors are repeated enough, they transform into habits. Here, it's important to remember the power of consistency. Just as a river shapes a landscape over time through persistent flow, consistent behaviors shape the culture of an organization.

Creating this environment also means providing the resources necessary for success. These resources can be tools, information, or access to expertise but should also include emotional and psychological support. Leaders must ensure that their teams not only have what they need to do their jobs but also feel secure in taking risks and making decisions. This support is part of the resources equation, facilitating an atmosphere where team members can experiment, learn from their mistakes, and innovate.

Moreover, the leader's role in this process-oriented approach is to monitor, guide, and adjust the environment and resources based on the team's performance and feedback. This adaptive leadership ensures that the team's needs are continually met, even as those needs evolve. It's about being responsive and proactive, not just setting up a one-time framework and stepping away.

Emphasizing that leaders should focus on creating conditions for growth rather than providing direct solutions reinforces the value of learning and development within the team. When team members solve problems themselves, they not only learn more effectively but also feel a greater sense of accomplishment and ownership over their work. This ownership is crucial for motivation and engagement, which are key drivers of performance.

Leadership is a strategic process of creating the right environment and providing adequate resources, designed to foster specific behaviors that evolve into productive habits, shaping a performance-driven culture. As leaders, our greatest contribution is not the solutions we offer but the self-sustaining system we build—that mathematical equation where process leads to behaviors, behaviors form habits, and habits culminate in a strong, resilient culture.

This process-oriented perspective shifts the focus from trying to embody an abstract ideal of leadership to executing well-defined actions that lead to success. It demystifies the concept and makes it accessible to anyone willing to learn and apply its principles.

Think of leadership not as constructing an elaborate mosaic from scratch each time, but rather as following a well-designed blueprint.

This blueprint, when followed, can lead to the construction of a robust and thriving organizational culture. Leadership, therefore, involves setting up systems—processes that ensure behaviors are not left to chance but are deliberately cultivated to foster a healthy and productive environment.

This foundational thinking is essential—it sets the stage for effective leadership—but it begs the question: where are the processes, and how do they come to life? This book serves as a practical guide to the structured art of leadership, presenting a set of actionable processes that can be consistently executed to drive key behaviors, form sustainable habits, and shape a culture of excellence.

Leadership isn't just about inspiration or vision; it's about creating systems that translate those ideals into measurable actions. That's where the mantra "what gets measured gets done" comes into play. By focusing on tangible, trackable actions and repeatable practices, leaders can move beyond theory to make real, impactful changes in their teams and organizations.

The processes outlined in this book are designed to empower leaders to take intentional steps toward building trust, aligning goals, and fostering accountability. Each process is a tool—not only for immediate results but also for creating long-term momentum. When leaders commit to measurable practices, they're not just managing—they're transforming their environment, driving meaningful change, and setting the foundation for a legacy of leadership by design.

Who This Book Is For?

This book is for anyone who wants to lead—or lead better. Whether you're an emerging leader stepping into your first leadership role, a seasoned leader refining your approach, or someone unexpectedly thrust into a position of responsibility, this book offers practical tools and guidance to help you navigate your leadership journey.

But more than that, this book is for organizations that lack a common operating model of leadership. Too often, leadership is left to chance—a vague, undefined concept that varies from one person to the next. Without a shared framework, how do we define what it means to lead? How do we train, measure, and grow leaders consistently and at scale?

Every company needs a clear and actionable leadership model—a framework of processes that provides structure, a shared language, and measurable outcomes for what leadership looks like in practice. This book delivers exactly that: a proven operating model that equips leaders with the tools they need to execute daily, align their efforts with organizational goals, and measure their performance.

A common leadership model is more than just a guide; it's the foundation for organizational success. It levels the playing field, ensuring all leaders operate from a shared baseline of expectations. With this foundation, companies can identify and develop high performers, support those who need growth, and foster a culture of continuous improvement. Without such a model, leadership becomes fragmented, inconsistent, and nearly impossible to measure.

This book isn't about abstract theories or one-size-fits-all solutions. It's about giving leaders a clear, actionable process to follow—a practical way to lead with both structure and humanity, and a system for measuring and improving leadership performance over time. Whether you're an individual leader striving for growth or an organization seeking a cohesive and effective leadership culture, this book is your guide to creating lasting impact.

Leading By Design, a Leadership Operating Model

Just as a computer needs an operating system to function, organizations need an operating system for leadership. **Leading By Design** is exactly that—a structured, scalable framework of processes that serves as the leadership operating model for any organization. It provides the foundation, processes, and tools necessary for leaders to align their efforts, execute effectively, and measure results.

Leading By Design isn't just about defining what good leadership looks like; it's about making it repeatable, teachable, and measurable. It's a system that turns the often ambiguous art of leadership into a structured process that can be scaled across teams and organizations. With this model, leaders gain clarity, teams find cohesion, and organizations thrive.

Why an Operating Model for Leadership Matters

Without a clear leadership framework, leadership becomes subjective, inconsistent, and often chaotic. Each leader interprets their role based on personal experience, resulting in fragmented approaches that frequently conflict or fail to deliver results. This lack of cohesion breeds confusion, inefficiency, and missed opportunities for growth.

An operating model for leadership changes the game. It ensures that everyone speaks the same language and operates from the same book. It provides clarity about what it means to lead, how to lead effectively, and how to measure leadership success. This common framework empowers organizations to align leaders at all levels, creating consistency and predictability in leadership outcomes.

When implemented as an organization's leadership operating model, **Leading By Design** transforms leadership from a personal skillset into an organizational capability. Here's how:

- **Establishing a Common Language:** By defining leadership in clear, measurable terms, Leading By Design ensures that all leaders—from emerging supervisors to seasoned executives—share a unified understanding of what leadership entails.
- **Creating Alignment:** The model provides a structured approach to align leadership practices with organizational goals. This

alignment fosters consistency across departments, enabling leaders to drive initiatives that support the broader vision.

- **Driving Measurable Outcomes:** Just as an operating system tracks performance through processes, Leading By Design enables organizations to evaluate leadership effectiveness. It ensures leaders are not just meeting expectations but exceeding them.
- **Problem Solving:** When a problem arises, you must have a process to point to and focus efforts on diagnosing the issue. With an operating model in place, you can ask, "Which part of the process failed or needs more attention?" This clarity allows for targeted solutions and continuous improvement.
- **Enabling Scalability:** Whether applied to a small team or a global enterprise, the framework is scalable, allowing organizations to maintain leadership excellence as they grow.
- **Supporting Development:** The model prioritizes leadership growth by identifying areas for improvement, providing tools for development, and fostering a feedback-rich culture that supports continuous learning.

Why Leading By Design Works

Leading By Design works because it is practical, measurable, and adaptable. It simplifies the complexities of leadership into actionable steps while maintaining the flexibility to adapt to an organization's unique needs. Just as an operating system allows a computer to function efficiently, Leading By Design creates the conditions for leadership to thrive within an organization.

By providing a clear framework, it eliminates the guesswork of leadership and creates a roadmap for success. Leaders are equipped to focus on their teams, build strong relationships, and deliver results. At the same time, organizations gain a consistent way to evaluate and improve leadership at every level.

Leading By Design is more than a framework; it is a philosophy that leadership should be both structured and human. The structure provides the stability and clarity leaders need to navigate their roles, while the focus on humanity ensures they lead with empathy, connection, and authenticity. Together, these elements create a model that not only drives results but also inspires people to bring their best selves to work.

By adopting Leading By Design as an operating model for leadership, organizations can create a culture of consistency, accountability, and growth. It becomes the foundation upon which leaders can build, innovate, and excel, ensuring that leadership is not just an individual effort but an organizational strength.

THE PARATUS LEADING BY DESIGN MODEL

Process creates Behaviors, Behaviors creates Habits, Habits creates Culture. Culture creates Performance.
— Robert Lee Barber

The **Leading By Design Model** by Paratus Consulting LLC encapsulates a comprehensive approach to leadership through a sequential model that builds upon itself. Each of the six quadrants in the model represents a distinct bucket of leadership concepts, processes, and tools, designed to enhance the efficacy and influence of leaders in any organizational context.

A Model for a Lifetime

Leadership is not static; it evolves as responsibilities grow. Whether you are leading a small project as a student, managing a team as a mid-level leader, or steering an organization as an executive, the **Leading By Design** model grows with you. It adapts to new challenges and contexts while providing a consistent process for success.

While this book hones in on the realities faced by entry to mid-level leaders, the model's principles remain universally applicable. It ensures that no matter where you are in your leadership journey, you have the tools to create meaningful impact.

By using this book alongside and possibly enhancing with the **Leading By Design workshops**, leaders can develop repeatable, scalable processes that align with the framework's principles. Together, these tools enable leaders to lead with clarity, consistency, and purpose, fostering a culture of accountability and success at every level. Each of the components in the model is designed to stack on one another and be sequential for planning and measuring purposes, but as you move through leadership you will access each as needed. Now lets begin to unpack each one of the components of the model.

1. Clarity of Purpose

Great leadership starts with clarity. It's the foundation where vision meets action. Leaders with clarity understand the "why" behind their role and connect it to the organization's vision. This alignment not only drives focus but inspires teams to rally around a shared purpose. Without clarity, leadership is aimless; with it, every decision and effort is rooted in meaning and direction.

How to Lead by Design: Use Clarity of Purpose to align personal and team goals with the organization's vision. Communicate this alignment regularly to keep your team focused on the bigger picture, and reinforce it by modeling purpose-driven decision-making in your daily leadership.

In the chapter for Clarity of Purpose we will unpack some key strategies on how to teach, challenge or role model with clarity of purpose. They include:

- **Aligning Personal and Organizational Vision:** How do your personal goals integrate with your company's vision? We'll explore how to achieve alignment and use it as a compass for decision-making.
- **Developing Interviewing Competencies:** Leadership starts with hiring. Learn how to assess talent beyond resumes to find individuals who align with your team's culture and goals.
- **Avoiding Common Leadership Mistakes:** Leadership isn't immune to pitfalls. From micromanaging to ignoring feedback, we'll break down the common traps and how to avoid them.
- **Building on Leadership Strengths for Team Success:** Everyone has unique strengths. Discover how to leverage yours to create high-performing, cohesive teams.

2. Setting Direction

Leadership without direction is chaos in disguise. Setting direction is about mapping the path forward—transforming lofty goals into actionable strategies that energize and align your team. It's where vision becomes reality, fueled by clear communication and relentless focus. Great leaders don't just point the way; they define it with precision and purpose.

How to Lead by Design: Use Setting Direction to define SMART goals for your team and communicate them with clarity. Create a roadmap for success, ensuring each team member knows their role in achieving the objectives. Regularly check progress and adjust direction to stay on course.

In the chapter for Setting Direction we will unpack some key strategies on how to teach, challenge, or role model for setting direction. They include:

- **Defining and Communicating SMART Goals:** Understand why vague goals fail and how to create objectives that are clear, measurable, and tied to broader organizational success.
- **Enhancing Communication Skills:** Effective communication isn't just about speaking; it's about being heard. Learn how to deliver your message with impact and clarity.
- **Supervising and Tracking Projects Effectively:** Leadership isn't about micromanaging—it's about creating systems that ensure progress without bottlenecks.
- **Managing Relationships Across the Organization:** Leadership is relational. Discover strategies to build influence and trust with peers, supervisors, and team members alike.

3. Consistent Execution

Execution is the grind of leadership—the daily discipline that turns plans into results. Consistent execution isn't glamorous, but it's essential. It's about prioritizing effectively, managing time like it's your most valuable asset, and saying "no" to distractions. Leaders who execute consistently build trust, maintain momentum, and prove that effort equals outcomes.

How to Lead by Design: Focus on daily prioritization, effective delegation, and time management to maintain consistent execution. Use tools like time-blocking and task-tracking to keep yourself and your team on target. Create a rhythm of accountability that reinforces reliability and builds trust.

In the chapter for Consistent Execution we will unpack some key strategies on how to teach, challenge, or role model for executing consistently. They include:

- **Prioritizing Tasks Using Effective Techniques:** Learn frameworks like the Eisenhower Matrix to triage tasks and stay focused on what truly matters.

- **Managing Time Efficiently and Saying "No":** Time is a finite resource. Master time-blocking and other techniques to maximize your productivity.
- **Delegating Tasks Wisely:** Delegation isn't just about offloading work; it's about empowering your team and building their skills.
- **Learning When and How to Professionally Decline Requests:** Saying "yes" to everything is a fast track to burnout. We'll cover how to decline requests without damaging relationships.

4. Connection

Leadership is a people business, and connection is its currency. It's the bridge between strategy and execution, the glue that turns teams into communities. Connection means building trust, fostering collaboration, and creating an environment where people feel heard, valued, and motivated. Without connection, leadership is mechanical; with it, it's magnetic.

How to Lead by Design: Build connection through meaningful one-on-one meetings, active listening, and open communication. Regularly engage your team by seeking their input and recognizing their contributions. Foster collaboration by creating a culture of trust and psychological safety.

In the chapter for Connection we will unpack some key strategies on how to teach, challenge, or role model for building community and connection. They include:

- **Building Rapport and Encouraging Open Communication:** Learn how to create psychological safety so your team feels heard and valued.
- **Motivating and Engaging Team Members:** Motivation isn't just about incentives; it's about aligning personal and team goals for shared success.

- **Addressing and Resolving Attitude Problems:** Toxic attitudes can derail a team. Discover strategies to address and resolve negativity constructively.

- **Implementing Continuous Feedback Mechanisms:** Feedback isn't just an annual event—it's a daily practice. Learn how to give and receive feedback that drives growth.

5. Compliance

Compliance isn't just about following the rules—it's about creating a foundation of integrity, fairness, and accountability. Leaders who prioritize compliance build trust with their teams and protect their organizations from unnecessary risks. It's not bureaucracy; it's leadership with a backbone. Playing by the rules isn't optional—it's how great leaders earn respect and build sustainable success.

How to Lead by Design: Use Compliance to establish clear expectations, enforce rules consistently, and model ethical behavior. Proactively communicate policies and the reasons behind them, and create a culture where integrity is non-negotiable.

In the chapter for Compliance we will unpack some key strategies on how to teach, challenge, or role model for ensuring accountability and adherence to how we do the work well. They include:

- **Knowing and Adhering to HR Laws and Policies:** Ignorance isn't an excuse. We'll cover the basics every leader needs to know to stay compliant.

- **Managing Performance Effectively:** Performance management isn't about micromanagement—it's about setting expectations and helping your team meet them.

- **Handling Exits and Transitions Within the Team:** Every team faces turnover. Learn how to handle departures with professionalism and respect.

- **Maintaining Compliance with Employment Standards:** Build a culture of fairness and consistency to protect both your team and your organization.

6. Go Forward Development

Leadership isn't just about today; it's about shaping tomorrow. Go Forward Development is where growth, mentorship, and succession planning come into play. It's about investing in your team's future and your own, ensuring the next generation of leaders is prepared to thrive. Great leaders don't just solve problems—they create legacies that last.

How to Lead by Design: Use Go Forward Development to prioritize growth—your own and your team's. Mentor emerging leaders, create opportunities for skill-building, and actively plan for succession. Make development a core part of your leadership strategy, ensuring your impact endures.

In the chapter for Go Forward Development we will unpack some key strategies on how to teach, challenge, or role model for ensuring growth and continued learning. They include:

- **Planning for Personal and Team Development:** Leadership development is intentional. Discover how to craft plans that drive growth.
- **Recognizing and Acting on Team Dynamics and Career Trajectories:** Understand your team's strengths, weaknesses, and potential to position them for success.
- **Implementing Mentorship Programs:** Mentorship isn't just nice to have; it's essential. Learn how to create programs that build future leaders.
- **Graduating Team Members to New Roles or Responsibilities:** Leadership is about building talent pipelines. Master the art of transitioning team members to roles where they can thrive.

A Model That Organizes Leadership Activities

One of the most powerful aspects of the **Leading By Design** model is how it groups the normal activities expected of a leader into a clear and structured cadence. Leaders often juggle a wide range of responsibilities, and this model helps them align these tasks with a repeatable, scalable process:

- **Daily Activities**: Leaders focus on activities such as defining priorities, connecting with team members, and maintaining alignment with organizational goals. Examples include morning check-ins, task prioritization, and quick feedback sessions.
- **Weekly Activities**: Each week, leaders assess progress toward goals, hold strategic one-on-one meetings, and address team challenges. These activities build momentum and ensure consistency in execution.
- **Quarterly Activities**: On a quarterly basis, leaders evaluate team performance, adjust goals based on evolving organizational needs, and engage in strategic planning to ensure alignment with long-term objectives.
- **Yearly Activities**: Annually, leaders participate in high-level planning, reflect on organizational culture and team development, and assess how their leadership has impacted overall performance.

By organizing leadership into these timeframes, the model ensures leaders can approach their responsibilities with clarity and intention. It creates a rhythm of leadership that is easy to replicate, scale, and measure.

Universal Principles for Every Leader

Now, it is important to recognize that what is taught under each component in this book is not fully comprehensive. We have identified key tactical activities for leaders within each component that are impactful and helpful in getting you started with Leading By Design. The strength of the **Leading By Design** model lies in its sequential, scalable, and repeatable framework. Each quadrant—**Clarity of Purpose**, **Setting Direction**, **Consistent Execution**, **Connection**, **Compliance**, and **Go Forward Development**—provides actionable strategies that group and organize the daily, weekly, quarterly, and yearly activities expected of a leader. These activities are broken into repeatable processes that are easy to communicate, measure, and scale across teams and organizations.

The model's principles are universal, making it adaptable to leaders at all levels and across any organizational context. It ensures leaders have a structured approach to the most critical aspects of their role:

- **Clarity of Purpose**: Helps leaders understand and articulate the "why" behind their actions, creating alignment and motivation at every level.
- **Setting Direction**: Enables leaders to communicate goals effectively, no matter the team size or complexity of the objective.
- **Consistent Execution**: Builds trust and momentum through reliability, accountability, and follow-through on commitments.
- **Connection**: Fosters relationships that drive engagement, collaboration, and shared purpose within teams.
- **Compliance**: Safeguards the integrity and alignment of leadership practices with ethical, legal, and organizational standards.
- **Go Forward Development**: Promotes continuous growth and adaptability through reflection, mentoring, and skill-building.

Each quadrant provides a roadmap for navigating leadership challenges, from managing team dynamics to driving strategic results, ensuring leaders can develop, execute, and refine their leadership consistently.

Does it work for any experience level?

What makes this model truly unique is its universal applicability. Whether you are an entry-level professional, a student leading a campus organization, a nonprofit volunteer, a senior executive at a Fortune 500 company, or anything in between, the Leading By Design model provides practical guidance tailored to your unique leadership challenges.

The Leading By Design model is a versatile operating system for leadership that applies across roles, levels, and industries. Whether you're a student leading peers, an executive guiding strategic initiatives, or a volunteer managing a nonprofit team, this model brings clarity and process to leadership. By integrating its components—Clarity of Purpose, Setting Direction, Consistent Execution, Connection, Compliance, and Go Forward Development—leaders can address their unique challenges while fostering growth and driving results.

For Student Leaders

Student leaders often step into roles with enthusiasm but lack the experience or framework to guide their efforts. The Leading By Design model equips them with a structured process to lead effectively by helping them articulate goals (Clarity of Purpose), outline actionable plans (Setting Direction), and build momentum through consistent habits (Consistent Execution).

Example: A student body president can use the model as a roadmap to align their team's vision with the school's broader vision, ensuring clarity and unity. By prioritizing Connection, they foster collaboration and belonging, while Compliance ensures adherence to policies and fair decision-making. Go Forward Development helps them mentor peers and build a legacy for future student leaders.

For Entry-Level Leaders

New professionals in entry-level roles often lead without formal authority, requiring them to influence and inspire through process and competence. The Leading By Design model empowers them to approach their tasks with confidence by integrating strategic planning, personal accountability, and relational excellence into their leadership.

Example: A marketing associate tasked with leading a project can use the model to ensure all components of the campaign are aligned with organizational goals (Clarity of Purpose), while Setting Direction helps them break the project into manageable steps. Consistent Execution keeps them on track with deadlines, and Connection ensures strong teamwork and collaboration. Compliance guarantees the project adheres to branding standards, and Go Forward Development helps them identify opportunities to improve their skills and contribute more effectively.

For Nonprofit and Volunteer Leaders

Nonprofit and volunteer leaders face unique challenges, such as managing limited resources and working with diverse teams. The Leading By Design model offers a holistic framework to streamline operations, inspire teams, and achieve vision-driven outcomes.

Example: A volunteer coordinator can use the model to clarify the organization's vision and set achievable goals for community programs (Clarity of Purpose and Setting Direction). They can foster team collaboration and a sense of purpose through Connection while ensuring operational and ethical standards are upheld with Compliance. Through Go Forward Development, they can empower volunteers to grow their skills, ensuring the sustainability of the organization's impact.

For Mature Leaders

Leaders with years of experience often face the challenge of maintaining energy, adapting to change, and inspiring the next generation of leaders. The Leading By Design model provides a comprehensive framework to bring purpose, structure, and adaptability to their leadership.

Example: A senior leader managing a well-established team can use the model to reassess and realign their department's goals with the evolving needs of the organization (Clarity of Purpose and Setting Direction). Consistent Execution helps maintain operational excellence, while Connection bridges generational gaps and fosters collaboration. Compliance ensures continued adherence to organizational values, and Go Forward Development enables them to mentor emerging leaders, ensuring their legacy and the organization's success endure.

For Senior Executives

Executives at the highest levels often manage complex challenges, such as driving large-scale change and aligning diverse teams. The Leading By Design model serves as an operating system to help them navigate these challenges with precision and purpose.

Example: A CEO leading a company through a merger can rely on the model to ensure the vision for the combined organization is clear and actionable (Clarity of Purpose). Setting Direction helps define integration priorities, while Consistent Execution ensures progress is steady and measurable. Connection fosters unity across teams, Compliance guarantees all processes align with legal and ethical standards, and Go Forward Development creates opportunities for long-term growth and innovation within the new organization.

How to Use Leading By Design Operating Model

Leadership is not a one-time achievement; it's a journey of continuous evolution. It requires ongoing learning, adaptation, and a deep understanding of yourself, your team, and the environment in which you operate. Whether you're encountering the Leading By Design

Operating Model for the first time, missed the related workshop, or are revisiting these concepts to strengthen your understanding, this book is designed to serve as both an introduction and an enhancement to the work we do at Paratus Consulting.

This book is not intended to replace the Leading By Design workshop or the value of partnering with Paratus Consulting LLC to fully install the model within your organization. Instead, it serves as a complement —a resource that primes you for deeper engagement or reinforces and enhances the strategies you've already explored with us. Think of it as your personal guide for integrating the Leading By Design Operating Model into your leadership journey.

Here, you'll find actionable tools and insights that make the abstract principles of leadership tangible and achievable. From developing processes that foster desirable behaviors to creating habits that shape culture, this book will help you translate leadership ideals into measurable results.

How to Approach This Book

Use It as an Introduction: If you're new to Leading By Design, this book provides a foundational understanding of the model's core components and principles. It's an entry point to learning how structure and humanity combine to create exceptional leadership.

Enhance Workshop Learning: For those who've attended the workshop, this book serves as a reinforcement tool. It expands on key concepts and provides additional context, examples, and exercises to deepen your understanding and application of the model.

Partner for Greater Impact: Use this book as a stepping stone to working with Paratus Consulting, where we guide organizations through the process of fully implementing the Leading By Design Operating Model. Together, we help align leadership practices with organizational goals for sustainable impact.

Apply It Daily: Leadership is a practice that evolves through consistent effort. This book offers guidance on how to integrate the Leading By Design principles into your everyday routine, helping you lead with clarity, execute with consistency, and build meaningful connections.

Measure and Reflect: One of the unique strengths of the Leading By Design Operating Model is its emphasis on measurability. Use the tools in this book to track your leadership performance over time, reflect on your progress, and adjust your approach to continue growing.

The Path from Process to Culture

As you navigate through this book, remember that effective leadership starts with clear processes and ends with the culture you create and sustain. Processes shape behaviors; behaviors form habits; habits define culture; and culture drives performance.

This book lays out this journey—offering frameworks to establish processes, build habits, and nurture a culture of accountability, growth, and collaboration. It equips you to begin the transformation, while the workshop and ongoing partnership with Paratus Consulting ensure the system is fully integrated into your organization.

A Primer for Leadership Excellence

Leadership isn't something to be studied in trait theory alone; it's something you do. Let this book be your introduction to the Leading By Design Operating Model or an enhancement to the work you've already started. Use it as a guide to turn leadership principles into actions, processes into habits, and goals into outcomes. Together with Paratus Consulting, this framework will help you and your organization thrive.

Each chapter of this book is organized around a component of the Leading By Design operating model, providing a clear and actionable framework for leadership. Within each chapter, you'll find processes, ideas, and tools to adopt and implement in your leadership journey. The structure is designed to guide you through understanding, internalizing, and applying each component effectively

Each page is an opportunity to inspire, challenge, and transform your approach to leading.

Embark on Your Leadership Journey

As you turn the pages of this book, remember that leadership is a continuous process of learning and growth. The path to becoming a great leader is perpetual, filled with challenges and opportunities that demand resilience, adaptation, and above all, a clear sense of purpose. Use this book to chart your course in the intricate world of leadership, where every day presents a new chance to lead by design—not by default.

Fundamentals of Leadership Within The Model

Before we conclude the model overview and dive into the details, let's unpack some fundamentals of leadership execution. You will see this again in the Connection component of the model. I call this the connective tissue of the **Leading by Design** model and its also how you will connect with your people as a part of what we call "Connective Intelligence (CI)". We will explore these fundamental pillars in depth in Chapter 6, **Connection**, where we'll discuss how they bring the model to life. However, it's important to plant the seeds here.

When I teach the **Leading by Design** model, a common question arises: "How do I do all this?" Most high-performing leaders want to get straight to the "doing" part of leading.

Within the model, all the concepts, processes, activities, programs, and tactical strategies can be executed through one or more of the fundamental ways we all lead: **We teach. We challenge. We role model.**

Leadership is expressed through these three core pillars—teaching, challenging, and role modeling. These roles are not separate from the **Leading by Design** model but are embedded within its execution. As leaders engage with each component—**Clarity of Purpose, Setting Direction, Consistent Execution, Connection, Compliance, and Go Forward Development**—they step into these roles to guide and empower their teams.

By understanding how these leadership roles integrate into the operating model, leaders can apply the framework in ways that resonate deeply with their teams and drive meaningful results. **Teaching, challenging, and role modeling** aren't just methods; they are the heart of how leadership is practiced and how the model is brought to life.

A Leader Teaches Within the Model

Teaching is critical to leadership and is woven into every component of the *Leading By Design* model. Leaders teach by providing knowledge, context, and the tools necessary for others to succeed. For instance:

- **Clarity of Purpose:** Leaders teach the "why" behind goals, ensuring the team understands the vision and how their work contributes.

- **Connection:** Teaching fosters understanding and builds trust by helping team members communicate effectively and collaborate meaningfully.

Example: When setting a new organizational vision, a leader uses teaching within Clarity of Purpose to help the team see the big picture and their role in achieving it. By teaching communication techniques through Connection, they ensure alignment and buy-in across the team.

A Leader Challenges Within the Model

Challenging is about pushing individuals and teams to grow, innovate, and achieve beyond their current limits. Leaders use challenging as a tool to activate components of the model:

- **Setting Direction:** Leaders challenge their teams to stretch their goals and take bold steps to achieve them.
- **Go Forward Development:** Challenging helps individuals step into new roles, build skills, and prepare for the future.

Example: A leader uses Setting Direction to challenge a team to pursue an ambitious project, encouraging innovative thinking and resilience. Within Go Forward Development, they challenge team members to step out of their comfort zones, fostering personal and professional growth.

A Leader Role Models Within the Model

Role modeling demonstrates leadership in action, setting an example for others to follow. This is central to the successful execution of the model:

- **Consistent Execution:** Leaders model discipline and accountability, showing how to meet deadlines and deliver results.
- **Compliance:** By adhering to ethical standards and organizational policies, leaders exemplify integrity and professionalism.

Example: A leader managing a high-pressure project models Consistent Execution by maintaining focus and prioritization, inspiring their team to do the same. Through Compliance, they set the standard for ethical behavior, ensuring the team stays aligned with organizational values.

How It All Fits Together

The *Leading By Design* model serves as a comprehensive operating system for leadership, while teaching, challenging, and role modeling are the methods by which leaders bring its components to life. Leaders who master these roles within the framework create clarity, build trust, inspire growth, and achieve sustainable success.

Leadership is not static, and neither is the *Leading By Design* model. By engaging in these roles within each component, leaders can adapt the model to any situation, empowering their teams and fostering long-term impact.

Summary

The Paratus Leading By Design Model offers a structured and adaptable framework that enables leaders at all levels to develop and refine their skills. Each quadrant—Clarity of Purpose, Setting Direction, Consistent Execution, Connection, Compliance, and Go Forward—builds on the others, providing a comprehensive roadmap for growth and effective management. What makes this model truly powerful is its flexibility; it can be easily tailored to the unique responsibilities and challenges of any leadership role, from entry-level professionals to senior executives, and across various working environments, including corporate, nonprofit, and volunteer settings.

For entry-level leaders, the model provides foundational strategies to establish credibility and build essential habits. Mid-level leaders can leverage the framework to manage teams, set strategic goals, and foster collaboration. Senior leaders and executives can use the model to refine organizational alignment, drive cultural change, and mentor future leaders.

The **Leading By Design Model** is more than a set of principles, processes, or checklists—it's a leadership operating system designed to guide you through the challenges and opportunities of leadership at every stage. In the chapters ahead, we will dive deeper into each quadrant of the model, exploring actionable strategies and real-world applications that will help you transform theory into practice.

Success Competencies

Lastly, a powerful complement to the Leading by Design Operating Model is Paratus Consulting's **Success Competency Model**. This model identifies the eight core competencies (**Growth Mindset, Self Actualization, Resilience, Boldness, Curiosity, Creativity, Focus, and Empathy**) that are essential for building and sustaining high-performing teams. These competencies go beyond technical skills; they encompass the traits, behaviors, and mindsets that drive collaboration, innovation, and consistent results.

Whether you're focused on hiring the right talent, developing your existing team, or fostering a culture of excellence, the Success Competency Model provides a clear framework to guide your efforts. Each competency has been meticulously researched and tested to ensure its relevance across industries and organizational types. By integrating this model into your leadership toolkit, you can take your team's performance to the next level.

For a deeper dive into these competencies and how they can transform your team, explore the Success Competency Model book, available online. It's a practical, actionable resource designed to help leaders align their teams with the principles of high performance, providing the tools needed to succeed in today's fast-paced business environment.

Now, Let's begin with the foundation of all great leadership: **Clarity of Purpose**. This is where leadership starts, where your vision takes shape, and where we set the stage for everything else to come.

Chapter 1
CLARITY OF PURPOSE

"When you have clarity of intention,
the universe conspires with you to make it happen."
— Fabienne Fredrickson

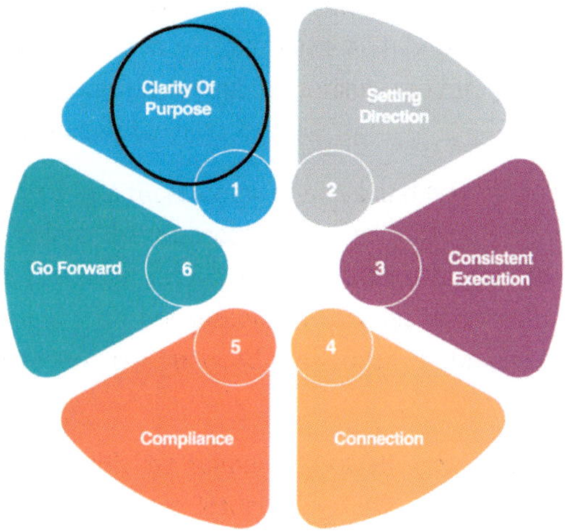

Imagine trying to steer a ship without a compass—constantly reacting to waves and winds but never charting a course. That's leadership without clarity: reactive, exhausting, and ultimately, directionless. **Clarity of Purpose** isn't just a buzzword; it's the foundation of effective leadership. It's what separates those who simply manage from those who truly lead.

This chapter isn't about lofty ideals or vague inspiration. It's about getting crystal clear on who you are as a leader, why you're here, and how to align your personal vision with your organization's vision. It's about understanding the difference between being the one doing the work and the one creating the conditions for success. True leadership isn't found in the weeds; it's rooted in perspective, purpose, and the ability to inspire others to follow.

Clarity of Purpose is your **North Star**. Without it, leadership becomes a foggy, frustrating grind. But with it, every decision and action aligns with a greater vision, driving not just results but trust, accountability, and impact. This chapter is your roadmap to stepping out of the weeds and into the clarity that defines great leadership.

At its core, Clarity of Purpose is about understanding who you are as a leader, where you're going, and why you're doing it. Most importantly, it's about knowing the difference between being a leader and an individual contributor. Confusing the two is like mistaking the conductor of an orchestra for the violinist—they both create music, but their roles couldn't be more different.

Leader vs. Individual Contributor

We begin our journey to Clarity of Purpose by focusing on the essential shift from being an individual contributor to embracing your role as a leader. Even senior leaders, despite years of experience, occasionally slip back into individual contributor mode—sometimes more often than they'd like to admit. Why? Because it feels good to do the work we've mastered. In high-pressure situations, reverting to the familiar can feel like the fastest way to regain control.

But here's the truth: transitioning from an individual contributor to a leader is one of the most significant shifts you'll make in your professional life. It's not just about a new title or a larger team—it's a complete transformation in mindset, responsibility, and perspective.

As an individual contributor, your focus is on executing specific tasks with precision and efficiency. Your success is measured by personal performance metrics: completing projects, solving technical problems, and achieving clearly defined objectives. But stepping into a leadership role broadens your scope dramatically. Leaders must go beyond technical expertise to develop a strategic vision that encompasses the entire team's operations.

This shift requires an elevated perspective, where the emphasis moves from task execution to goal setting, strategy creation, and aligning the efforts of a diverse group to achieve larger organizational objectives.

Never underestimate your ability to slip back into your high-performing individual contributor habits.

The Journey from Task-Oriented to Vision-Oriented

The transition from being task-oriented to vision-oriented isn't just about changing how you work; it's about fundamentally rethinking how you approach work. Leaders must cultivate the ability to look beyond immediate deliverables and focus on the long-term impacts of their team's efforts.

This includes fostering a positive team dynamic, motivating and developing team members, and aligning the team's output with the strategic goals of the organization. Instead of solely celebrating individual accomplishments, leaders evaluate success through the lens of team performance and the overall health of the organization.

Leadership also brings complexity: resolving conflicts, managing diverse personalities, and inspiring the team toward shared successes. It's no longer about what *you* can do—it's about what you can enable others to do. This requires developing new skills like effective communication, empathy, and decision-making that balances the needs of various stakeholders.

Conceptual Shift in Responsibilities

The role shift from individual contributor to leader involves two major changes:

1. **From Execution to Strategy**
    - **Individual Contributor:** Focuses on completing specific tasks efficiently and effectively. Success is measured by personal achievements and adherence to technical standards.
    - **Leader:** Concentrates on the big picture, devising strategies that support the organization's objectives. Success is measured by the ability to guide the team toward collective goals.
2. **From Personal Metrics to Team Dynamics**
    - **Individual Contributor:** Operates within defined roles, with performance metrics based on individual output and skill proficiency.
    - **Leader:** Manages and nurtures team interactions and morale, ensuring that team dynamics contribute positively to the organization's success. Performance metrics include team productivity, cohesion, and the ability to resolve conflicts.

Historical and Trend Insights

Historically, the transition from individual contributor to leader has been one of the most challenging career shifts due to a lack of formal training in leadership skills. For decades, individuals were promoted based on technical expertise, often without consideration for interpersonal or strategic capabilities.

Over time, organizations have recognized this gap and increasingly invest in leadership development programs to prepare individuals for these roles.

Recent Trends:

- Emotional intelligence (EQ) is now a critical focus for effective leadership, emphasizing the importance of self-awareness and empathy.
- Adaptive leadership is gaining traction as leaders are expected to thrive in dynamic, rapidly changing environments.
- Continuous learning is a must, with leadership roles evolving to require more diverse and flexible skill sets.

Examples

A Good Example:

A mid-20th-century manufacturing company promoted a skilled engineer renowned for problem-solving. Instead of throwing her into the deep end, they enrolled her in a six-month leadership training program. She learned strategic planning, team management, and conflict resolution, resulting in a smooth transition and a more productive department.

A Bad Example:

In the early 2000s, a software development company promoted their best coder to team lead without any leadership training. While technically brilliant, he lacked interpersonal skills and struggled to manage his team, resulting in high turnover and missed project deadlines. The company failed to address this gap, leading to team morale issues and costly delays.

The Difference Between Leading and Doing

Here's the hard truth: if you're buried in the weeds of every project, you're not leading—you're managing. And while managing is critical in some organizations, leadership operates at a higher altitude. Leaders see the big picture, connect the dots, and chart the course for the team.

Individual contributors excel at executing tasks; leaders excel at **enabling others** to execute those tasks effectively.

The moment you step into a leadership role, your job shifts from **"doing the work"** to **"creating the conditions where others can do the work."** Leaders with clarity know how to delegate without feeling threatened. They understand that their value comes from setting direction, removing obstacles, and aligning the team with a shared vision—not from micromanaging or hoarding tasks to prove their worth.

Strategies for a Successful Transition

1. **Developing Strategic Oversight**
    - **Training:** Participate in leadership workshops and seminars to build skills in strategic planning and vision setting.
    - **Mentorship:** Seek guidance from experienced leaders to gain practical insights into managing and leading teams.
2. **Fostering Effective Team Dynamics**
    - **Communication Skills:** Invest in negotiation, conflict resolution, and effective communication training.
    - **Team-Building Activities:** Regularly organize activities that enhance trust and collaboration within the team.
3. **Aligning with Organizational Goals**
    - **Alignment Workshops:** Join sessions designed to connect team goals with the organization's broader vision.
    - **Regular Feedback:** Create a system of continuous feedback from both upper management and team members to ensure alignment and adjust strategies as needed.

Connecting with the Organization's Vision

Now that we've established clarity around your role as a leader—and left behind the individual contributor mindset that earned you the leadership position—it's time to focus on your most critical responsibility: connecting the organization's vision to your own and to your team members'.

Clarity of Purpose isn't just about understanding your personal vision as a leader—it's about aligning that vision with the broader vision of the organization. Without this connection, leadership becomes disconnected and directionless. If you don't know **why** you're here, how can you possibly inspire your team to engage with the organization's vision?

True leadership begins with understanding your own **"why"**—the reason you show up, the purpose that drives you—and using that clarity to help others discover theirs. It's about translating the organizational vision into something tangible and personal for both you and your team. When you achieve this alignment, you create a powerful force that drives engagement, motivation, and collective success.

Ask yourself:

- Why am I in this role?
- How does my personal vision connect with the organization's vision?
- What do I want to achieve here, and how does it contribute to the bigger picture?

When leaders know their own "why," they can lead with authenticity. They're not just giving orders—they're connecting their team's efforts to something meaningful. Without this connection, leadership becomes transactional rather than transformational. A leader who lacks clarity about their purpose will never ask their team members about theirs, and that's where the disconnect begins.

Aligning Personal Vision with Organizational Vision

Great leaders have personal visions that energize them. But the secret sauce is aligning that vision with the organization's vision. When those two align, magic happens. You're no longer just clocking in; you're inspired and inspiring. Your purpose resonates with the company's, and that alignment becomes contagious, sparking motivation throughout your team.

When leaders connect their "why" with the organization's vision, they pave the way for their team to do the same. A team that knows its purpose doesn't just work harder—it works smarter, more cohesively, and with a sense of ownership.

Leveraging Your Strengths to Build Teams

Clarity of Purpose also means understanding your own strengths—and, equally important, your weaknesses. Leadership isn't about pretending to have all the answers; it's about assembling a team of people who can fill the gaps, challenge your perspective, and complement your skills.

This requires self-awareness, self actualization, and humility. Leaders who know their strengths and can double down on them while leaning on their team for support in areas where they're less effective. This not only creates a stronger team dynamic but also fosters trust and empowerment. Your job isn't to be the smartest person in the room; it's to **build a room full of smart people** who can achieve great things together.

Clarity Drives Purpose and Accountability

When leaders are clear about their purpose, their teams follow suit. This clarity cascades through the organization, aligning efforts, reducing confusion, and fostering accountability. Everyone understands not only what they're doing but why it matters.

Clarity of Purpose isn't just a nice-to-have; it's a non-negotiable. It's the first step toward becoming a leader who inspires, empowers, and drives meaningful results. Get this part right, and everything else begins to fall into place.

The Perfect Leader vs. The Perfect Team Member

A wonderful exercise is to create clarity around the vision of the perfect leader and team member. Too often, leaders and organizations lack a defined picture of what these roles should ideally look like, leaving teams to operate without a clear standard or direction. Effective leadership starts with crafting this vision and sharing it with your team.

The perfect leader isn't someone without flaws—it's someone who understands their strengths and weaknesses and knows how to balance them. A great leader communicates clearly, demonstrates empathy, and inspires their team through consistent actions that align with the organization's culture and goals. They aren't focused on perfection; they're focused on progress, authenticity, and impact.

Similarly, the ideal team member isn't just technically competent; they embody adaptability, collaboration, and alignment with the team's values. They embrace feedback as an opportunity to grow, take initiative when opportunities arise, and prioritize the collective success of the team over personal recognition.

By defining and articulating what the "perfect" leader and team member look like, leaders establish a clear standard that drives cohesion and excellence. This clarity informs hiring decisions, guides professional development, and anchors performance management, ensuring every decision contributes to the team's long-term success.

Exercise: Crafting Your Vision of the Perfect Leader and Team Member

Take a moment to reflect on the traits, behaviors, and values that define leadership and teamwork in your organization. Use the following questions to create an avatar for your ideal leader and team member:

1. **The Perfect Leader**
    - What three traits are non-negotiable for a great leader in your organization?
    - How should the perfect leader handle conflict, setbacks, or uncertainty?
    - What actions would a great leader take daily to inspire and motivate their team?
    - How does the ideal leader embody the organization's vision and values?
2. **The Perfect Team Member**
    - What specific skills or attributes make a team member indispensable?
    - How does the perfect team member contribute to a positive team dynamic?
    - What behaviors would make this team member stand out during challenging times?
    - How should they approach collaboration, feedback, and continuous learning?

By answering these questions, you'll develop a clear vision of the qualities you value most in leaders and team members. This vision can serve as a guiding framework for hiring, coaching, and building a culture where excellence thrives.

Transitioning from individual contributor to leader is more than a career milestone—it's a transformation in how you think, work, and inspire others. By understanding the shifts in responsibilities, recognizing common pitfalls, and embracing strategies for success, you can make this transition with confidence and clarity.

Leadership isn't about doing more work; it's about enabling more success. By stepping into this role with intention and purpose, you can drive not just your team's performance but their growth and engagement, setting the stage for lasting impact.

From Vision to Action

Once you've completed your prototypes, use them to take actionable steps:

1. **Assess Your Team**: Compare your team members to the "perfect team member" strawman. Identify gaps and areas for growth. Use this as a starting point for development plans, mentoring, or performance reviews.
2. **Guide Hiring Decisions**: Use your perfect team member prototype as a framework for recruiting and interviewing candidates, ensuring alignment with the team's needs and culture.
3. **Develop Yourself**: Compare your leadership style to the "perfect leader" strawman. Identify areas where you can grow and set specific goals to bridge the gap.

This exercise is not about perfection—it's about clarity. By defining your ideal leader and team member, you create a roadmap for growth, ensuring every decision you make as a leader is aligned with the culture and goals of your organization.

Leading with Vision and Company Culture

It never surprises me when teaching this portion of the model when I get the questions, "How do we lead with vision?" Effective leaders are visionaries who align their teams around a shared purpose and goal. Leading with vision involves more than simply articulating organizational objectives; it requires weaving these goals into the fabric of everyday activities, decisions, and behaviors. A clear and consistently communicated vision serves as a north star, guiding individual and collective efforts toward success. Company culture, in turn, forms the framework within which the team operates, shaping how the vision is experienced and enacted. Together, vision and culture create the foundation for a high-performing, engaged team.

Know and Share Your Vision

To lead with vision effectively, a leader must first know their own professional and personal vision. What drives you as a leader? What legacy do you want to leave, both within your organization and in your life? Taking time to define these answers is critical, as your personal vision provides the passion and energy necessary to inspire others.

Equally important is a deep understanding of the company's vision. Why does the organization exist, and how does its purpose connect with its long-term goals? Leaders who can internalize and articulate the organization's vision provide a clear and compelling reason for team members to rally behind their leadership.

However, it's not enough to know these visions personally. Great leaders share their own vision and the organization's vision frequently with their teams. This could take the form of storytelling during team meetings, tying day-to-day actions to the broader purpose, or recognizing individual contributions as part of a greater whole. When leaders make these connections explicit, they reinforce a sense of meaning and alignment.

Create that "Asking" Culture

A leader who hasn't done the deep work of defining their own personal and professional vision will struggle—if not outright fail—to build a culture where their team members feel valued, connected, and inspired. Why? Because you cannot ask others to explore their purpose when you haven't clarified your own.

If you, as a leader, cannot clearly articulate why you are in your role, what drives you to lead, and how your personal motivations align with the organization's vision, you will face the ultimate barrier to fostering an asking culture. The number one reason most leaders don't ask their teams about their motivations is simple—they haven't settled it for themselves. And without clarity, leadership defaults to authority rather than influence.

The Difference Between "Telling" and "Asking" Cultures

Without this personal clarity, organizations often become "telling cultures" by default—environments where the leader directs and the team complies. "Do this because I said so." This approach can achieve short-term results, but it lacks depth. It stifles creativity, limits long-term performance, and fails to engage people in a meaningful way. A telling culture demands action but rarely inspires ownership or loyalty.

Contrast that with an "asking culture"—a dynamic where leaders actively seek to understand their team members' personal and professional aspirations. It's about aligning individual motivations with organizational goals and creating a space where people feel genuinely valued for who they are, not just what they do. Leaders in asking cultures empower their teams to bring their best because they've taken the time to explore what drives them individually.

I will never forget a conversation I had with a CEO who was almost allergic to the idea of fostering an "asking" culture around team members' personal and professional aspirations. We have a workshop called "CONNECT for Teams", designed to shift professional development out of the traditional one-on-one setting between team members and leaders and into a professional group environment. In this setting, entire teams engage in professional development together, including creating their own personal and professional vision statements.

During a discussion with this particular CEO, she expressed concern, saying, "But what if they tell me they want to leave?"

I responded, "Wouldn't you want to know that now?"

If your goal is to create an environment where people bring their best every day—not just out of obligation but out of genuine connection to the work—clarity of purpose must come first. And it starts with the leader knowing their own "why" and then helping others discover theirs.

Clarifying Your Own Vision: The Foundation for Leading by Design

Before you can create a culture where others feel comfortable sharing their purpose, you need to go through the process yourself. Ask:

Why am I leading here?

How does my personal vision connect to the organization's vision?

What drives me to continue leading this team?

Am I clear on how my personal success aligns with the team's success?

When you've done this work—and can communicate it clearly—you'll be equipped to ask the same from your team. Leadership influence multiplies when leaders model self-awareness and personal alignment with the broader vision.

Creating an "Asking" Culture as Process

An asking culture isn't built on one-off conversations. It requires intentional, ongoing effort and a commitment to making it part of your leadership rhythm. Here's how you can start building it:

Consistent Curiosity: Regularly engage your team with meaningful questions about their professional and personal growth. "What motivates you in this role?" "Where do you want to grow this year?"

One-on-One Conversations: Move beyond surface-level check-ins. Ask questions about long-term goals, personal development, and how they feel connected (or disconnected) from the organization's vision.

Embed It in Reviews and Feedback: Use performance reviews as opportunities for deeper dialogue. Make development conversations just as important as performance metrics.

Model the Behavior: Share your own motivations openly. When leaders model vulnerability and clarity of purpose, it sets the expectation for others to do the same.

Align Roles with Purpose: Help team members see the direct link between their day-to-day responsibilities and the larger company vision. Show them how their contributions matter.

But What About When "Telling" Is Necessary?

You might be wondering, "Aren't there times when a leader needs to be directive?" Absolutely. In moments of crisis, during high-stakes decisions, or when immediate action is required, directive leadership plays a role. However, it should not be your default approach.

The highest-performing organizations maintain an asking culture as the norm because it creates buy-in, accountability, and long-term trust. Telling should be a tool, not a leadership style.

Clarity of Purpose in an Asking Culture

At its core, an asking culture creates clarity—for the leader, the team, and the organization as a whole. When you have clarity on your own purpose, you're better positioned to help your team clarify theirs. And when every person in the organization understands both the "why" and the "how" behind the work, execution transforms. Teams move from compliance to commitment. From reactive to proactive. From performing tasks to pursuing a shared vision.

Leadership isn't just about managing performance—it's about unlocking potential. And that starts with the courage to ask, listen, and connect.

Embodying Vision Through Culture

Company culture is the living expression of organizational values and vision supported by the processes. Effective leaders embody and reinforce this culture through their actions and decisions through the processes given a priority. Whether it's recognizing behaviors that align with company values, modeling accountability, or encouraging collaboration, leaders set the tone for the culture they wish to cultivate.

When leaders consistently demonstrate the connection between vision and culture, they create a cohesive environment where team members feel aligned and empowered. This connection is reinforced through rituals and practices that bring the vision to life—whether through celebrations of achievements, team-building activities, or regular communication of successes tied to the company's goals.

The Leader's Role

Ultimately, a leader's role in providing clarity of purpose through vision and culture is foundational to team and organizational success. By knowing and sharing their own vision, fostering an "asking" culture, and connecting individual goals with organizational objectives, leaders create an environment where people feel inspired and valued. When vision is clearly communicated and embedded into the culture, it becomes a powerful force that unites, motivates, and drives sustained performance.

Tactical Strategies and Processes for Leading with Vision and Fostering Culture

While leading with vision and fostering culture might sound like a grand endeavor, the key lies in daily, intentional processes and actions that embed these principles into your leadership practice. Here are practical strategies and processes that leaders can use to make their vision and culture come alive in their teams every day:

1. Start Meetings with Vision Alignment

Every meeting is an opportunity to remind your team of the bigger picture. Begin with a brief statement that ties the meeting's purpose back to the organizational vision or values. For example:

- "As we discuss this quarter's sales strategy, let's remember our commitment to delivering unparalleled customer value."
- "Today's project update ties directly into our goal of becoming the industry leader in innovation by 2025."

This practice reinforces alignment and ensures daily tasks remain connected to long-term goals.

2. Share Personal Vision Moments

Set aside time during team meetings or one-on-ones to share how your personal vision aligns with the work at hand. For example, you might say:

- "I've always been passionate about creating spaces where people can thrive, and that's why I'm excited about the employee development initiatives we're working on." Sharing these insights provides authenticity and helps team members see your leadership as purposeful and grounded.

3. Engage in "Vision Check-Ins" with Your Team

Incorporate questions about personal and professional aspirations into one-on-ones. These conversations don't need to be formal but should be consistent. Ask:

- "What's one thing you're excited to achieve this year?"
- "How does your current role help you get closer to your career goals?"
- "What's one area where you'd like to grow that aligns with our vision?"

These questions foster a culture of connection and show that you value your team members' aspirations.

4. Practice Vision Storytelling

Regularly tell stories that illustrate the company's vision in action. Highlight examples where individuals or teams exemplify organizational values or achieve goals that align with the broader vision. For instance:

- Share how a specific project made an impact on a customer, tying it back to the company's core purpose.
- Recognize a team member whose actions embodied the cultural value of collaboration or innovation.

Storytelling helps abstract visions feel tangible and achievable.

5. Use a Vision Journal

Maintain a simple vision journal where you jot down examples of how your daily work connects to your professional and personal vision and the company's vision. At the end of the day, reflect on:

- What actions did I take that supported my vision?
- How did I model the company's values today?

- What connections did I draw between team goals and the broader vision?

This habit helps leaders stay mindful and intentional about their impact.

6. Create Vision Boards for the Team

Encourage team members to create individual and collective vision boards that showcase personal goals, team goals, and connections to the company's vision. Display these boards in shared spaces or virtually. This visual representation reinforces alignment and serves as a constant reminder of purpose.

7. Celebrate Connections in Daily Interactions

Find ways to tie daily wins to the company vision and individual goals. For example:

- "Great work closing that deal! It's a perfect example of how we're driving toward our vision of becoming the preferred partner for sustainable solutions."
- "Your attention to detail on this report showcases how our team contributes to building trust with our clients."

Daily acknowledgment of these connections creates a culture of recognition and alignment.

8. Implement "Vision Moments" in Team Meetings

Dedicate 5–10 minutes in team meetings for a "Vision Moment," where you:

- Share a brief story that illustrates the vision in action.
- Ask team members to share how their work ties to the company's goals.
- Discuss a specific cultural value and brainstorm how the team can live it out in their current projects.

These moments ensure vision and culture are part of everyday team conversations.

9. Schedule Daily "Walk and Talk" Check-Ins

Take time each day to walk around (or virtually connect with remote teams) and check in informally with team members. Use this time to ask about their progress, challenges, and aspirations. For example:

- "How are you feeling about your goals this week?"
- "Is there anything you'd like to discuss that could help you align more with our vision?"

These informal touchpoints build trust and reinforce a connection to the vision.

10. Model the Culture You Want to Build

The most effective way to foster company culture is to live it yourself. Each day, demonstrate the values you want to see in your team:

- Show integrity by following through on commitments.
- Foster collaboration by openly seeking and valuing input.
- Encourage innovation by celebrating creative ideas and risk-taking.

When your team sees you consistently embodying the vision and culture, they're more likely to follow suit.

Daily Checklist for Vision and Culture

To keep these strategies and processes top of mind, incorporate a daily checklist into your routine:

1. Did I align today's tasks or meetings with our vision?
2. Did I share a story or example of our vision or values in action?
3. Did I ask at least one team member about their personal or professional aspirations?

4. Did I recognize a team member's work in connection to our goals?

5. Did I model the values I want to see in my team?

By embedding these strategies into your daily leadership practice, you'll create a team environment where vision and culture are not just words on a wall but living, breathing parts of your organization's DNA.

Incorporating vision and culture into daily leadership practice is not a one-time effort but a continuous journey that requires intentionality and consistency. When leaders take deliberate steps to connect their own vision, the organization's vision, and their team members' goals, they create a powerful sense of purpose that drives engagement and performance. By fostering an environment where vision is shared, culture is embodied, and aspirations are supported, leaders not only build alignment but also inspire their teams to contribute their best every day. Leading with vision and culture transforms ordinary work into extraordinary impact, empowering individuals and teams to achieve greatness together.

Remember culture begins as a process. Leading with vision is a process you can install.

Common Mistakes and Erosion of Clarity of Purpose

Leadership is full of landmines. Even the most experienced leaders can stumble into pitfalls that don't just slow progress—they actively erode **Clarity of Purpose**. And when clarity is lost at the top, the ripple effects are felt throughout the organization and team. Ambiguity spreads, trust weakens, and alignment crumbles.

The truth is, clarity isn't just a personal leadership process or pursuit—it's the lifeblood of an effective organization. Without it, teams lose focus, priorities get muddled, and the culture veers into chaos. To lead with clarity, leaders must first understand what takes it away and learn how to avoid those traps.

Mistake #1: Micromanagement

Micromanagement doesn't just stifle creativity—it clouds organizational clarity. When leaders hover over every detail, teams are left second-guessing their own decisions. Instead of focusing on their roles, team members waste energy trying to anticipate what their leader wants. This lack of autonomy muddles priorities and slows down progress.

How It Erodes Clarity:

- Teams are unsure of their responsibilities and boundaries.
- Leaders become bottlenecks, delaying decisions and creating confusion.
- Organizational priorities take a back seat to the leader's minute-by-minute oversight.

Proactive Processes to Avoid This Mistake:

- **Empower Team Members:** Define clear roles and responsibilities, allowing team members to take ownership of their work.
- **Focus on Big-Picture Outcomes:** Set expectations for results rather than processes, giving teams the flexibility to execute.
- **Support, Don't Control:** Provide resources and guidance upfront, then step back and let your team lead within their lanes.

Mistake #2: Lack of Vision

Without a clear vision, leaders set their teams adrift. A leader who fails to articulate the "why" behind goals leaves their team in a fog, unsure of how their work contributes to the bigger picture. This lack of direction doesn't just confuse the team—it leads to inefficiencies and misaligned efforts that hurt the entire organization.

How It Erodes Clarity:

- Team members lack a unifying purpose, leading to disengagement.
- Resources are misallocated to low-priority tasks.
- The organization's culture becomes reactive rather than intentional.

Proactive Processes to Avoid This Mistake:

- **Define the Vision:** Create a compelling vision that aligns with organizational goals and values.
- **Communicate Regularly:** Reiterate the vision in meetings, one-on-ones, and updates to keep it front and center.
- **Tie Tasks to Purpose:** Help team members see how their individual contributions align with the broader vision.

Mistake #3: Avoiding Difficult Conversations

When leaders avoid tough conversations, problems fester and grow. Conflict remains unresolved, negative behaviors go unchecked, and trust erodes. This not only creates confusion within the team but also undermines clarity for the entire organization. Teams begin to question whether standards are real or negotiable, leading to inconsistency and frustration.

How It Erodes Clarity:

- Expectations become murky when issues aren't addressed directly.
- Teams lose confidence in leadership's willingness to uphold standards.
- Cultural norms shift toward avoidance rather than accountability.

Proactive Processes to Avoid This Mistake:

- **Address Issues Early:** Nip conflicts in the bud before they escalate into larger problems.

- **Focus on Behavior, Not Personality:** Keep conversations professional and centered on actions, not individuals.
- **Foster a Culture of Feedback:** Normalize open communication so tough conversations become easier over time.

Mistake #4: Overpromising and Under-Delivering

A leader who overpromises erodes both their credibility and the team's confidence. When commitments aren't met, the organization's priorities become unclear, and trust in leadership diminishes. This creates a culture of uncertainty, where team members doubt whether goals are achievable—or worth striving for.

How It Erodes Clarity:

- Teams don't know which promises to prioritize.
- Trust in leadership weakens, leading to disengagement.
- Organizational goals lose credibility when they're consistently unmet.

Proactive Processes to Avoid This Mistake:

- **Be Realistic:** Set achievable goals that align with available resources and timelines.
- **Communicate Transparently:** If circumstances change, update your team immediately with a clear explanation.
- **Underpromise and Overdeliver:** Build trust by consistently exceeding expectations rather than falling short.

Mistake #5: Failing to Delegate

When leaders hoard tasks, clarity vanishes—both for the leader and the team. Leaders become overwhelmed and lose sight of strategic priorities, while team members are left underutilized and unclear about their roles. This creates confusion across the board, hindering both individual and organizational performance.

How It Erodes Clarity:

- Leaders become bogged down in minutiae, neglecting strategic vision.
- Team members don't understand their value or responsibilities.
- Organizational momentum slows as decision-making bottlenecks form.

Proactive Processes to Avoid This Mistake:

- **Know Your Team:** Match tasks to team members' strengths and growth areas.
- **Set Clear Expectations:** Outline what needs to be done, why it matters, and what success looks like.
- **Trust and Verify:** Empower your team while scheduling regular check-ins to ensure progress.

Mistake #6: Neglecting Personal Development

When leaders stop investing in themselves, their ability to bring clarity to the team diminishes. Leaders who stagnate fail to adapt to new challenges, leaving their teams rudderless in the face of change. This lack of personal growth sends the message that learning and improvement aren't valued—creating a ripple effect across the organization.

How It Erodes Clarity:

- Teams are left without direction when leaders fail to evolve.
- Organizational culture shifts toward complacency rather than growth.
- Blind spots remain unaddressed, leading to repeated mistakes.

Proactive Processes to Avoid This Mistake:

- **Make Learning a Priority:** Dedicate time to personal development through courses, books, and mentorship.
- **Seek Feedback:** Regularly ask for input from your team and peers to uncover blind spots.
- **Lead by Example:** Show your team that growth is a lifelong pursuit by embracing new challenges and learning opportunities.

Clarity as the Leader's Compass

Each of these mistakes chips away at the clarity that is so vital to effective leadership. Whether it's micromanaging, neglecting vision, or avoiding hard conversations, these pitfalls muddy the waters, leaving teams uncertain and organizations unfocused.

But when leaders prioritize clarity—by aligning their actions with their purpose, addressing issues head-on, and clarity through process—they create a ripple effect that transforms their teams and organizations. Clear leadership brings clear results.

So here's the challenge: Take a moment to reflect. Which of these mistakes might be clouding your clarity? And more importantly, how will you course-correct to bring focus and intention back to your leadership?

Clear Communication: The Foundation of Success

It's one thing to have clarity for yourself, but what about everyone else? Leadership isn't a solo act—it's a team effort. And for the team to succeed, clear communication is non-negotiable.

Clear communication is the bedrock of a successful team. Communication creates trust, alignment, and fosters collaboration. Without it, misunderstandings arise, productivity stalls, and morale takes a nosedive. People can't perform at their best when they're left guessing about their roles, responsibilities, or how their work fits into the bigger picture.

Effective communication bridges the gap. It ensures that every team member understands not only what they need to do but why it matters. It ties individual efforts to the organization's larger vision, creating alignment, purpose, and focus. When everyone is on the same page, teams move faster, make better decisions, and achieve results that no individual could accomplish alone.

Communication isn't just about talking—it's about listening, engaging, and making sure that your message is clear and understood. It's a connective tissue that holds great teams together and enables them to thrive. So what are some good strategies for clear communications around vision?

Processes for Clear Communication:

1. **Set Expectations Early and Often**: Clearly define roles, responsibilities, and performance standards at the outset of projects. Use tools like role matrices or project charters to avoid ambiguity.

2. **Conduct Regular Check-Ins**: Hold frequent one-on-one and team meetings to provide updates, clarify priorities, and address any misalignments.

3. **Encourage Open Dialogue**: Create an environment where team members feel comfortable asking questions, seeking clarification, and providing feedback without fear of judgment.

4. **Leverage Multiple Channels**: Use a mix of communication methods—email, video calls, in-person meetings, or collaboration tools like Slack or Teams—to ensure messages reach everyone effectively.

Strong Trust and Mutual Respect: The Glue That Holds Teams Together

Trust and respect form the emotional foundation of successful teams. When team members feel safe to express their ideas, voice concerns, and take risks, they are more engaged, innovative, and collaborative. Building trust requires leaders to model integrity, empathy, and reliability consistently.

Processes to Foster Trust and Respect:

1. **Model Vulnerability and Transparency**: Share your challenges and decision-making processes with the team. Demonstrating that you're human encourages openness and trust.

2. **Recognize and Value Contributions**: Publicly acknowledge individual and team efforts, emphasizing how their work aligns with organizational goals.

3. **Address Conflicts Promptly and Fairly**: Tackle disagreements head-on with a solutions-focused mindset. Show fairness in mediating disputes to maintain mutual respect.

4. **Invest in Relationships**: Spend time understanding your team members on a personal level. Knowing their aspirations, challenges, and motivations fosters a deeper connection.

Alignment with Vision and Goals: The North Star

Teams perform best when their efforts are clearly aligned with the organization's vision and objectives. Alignment provides purpose, direction, and a shared sense of achievement. When team members understand how their daily tasks contribute to the bigger picture, they feel more motivated and engaged.

Processes to Build Alignment:

1. **Reiterate the Vision Regularly**: Start meetings by connecting discussions back to the team's goals or the company's vision, keeping the vision at the forefront.

2. **Connect Individual Roles to Goals**: Help each team member see how their unique contributions impact the team's and organization's success.

3. **Measure Progress Against Goals**: Use dashboards, scorecards, or regular updates to track and celebrate progress, ensuring everyone stays aligned and motivated.

4. **Empower Decision-Making Within the Vision**: Encourage team members to make decisions within the framework of the company's vision and values, fostering ownership and accountability.

Building a Culture of Collaboration and Growth

Beyond communication, trust, and alignment, fostering a successful team involves creating an environment that encourages collaboration and personal development. Leaders can cultivate this culture by prioritizing engagement and growth.

Foster Collaboration:

- **Break Down Silos**: Promote cross-functional teamwork to share ideas and solutions across different areas of expertise.

- **Facilitate Knowledge Sharing**: Create opportunities for team members to share skills and insights through peer mentoring or collaborative workshops.

- **Celebrate Team Wins**: Recognize collective achievements, not just individual ones, to reinforce the value of collaboration.

Encourage Growth:

- **Invest in Development**: Offer opportunities for training, mentoring, and skill-building to help team members advance their careers.
- **Create Stretch Opportunities**: Assign challenging projects that push team members out of their comfort zones and encourage growth.
- **Provide Constructive Feedback**: Deliver regular feedback that helps team members refine their skills and gain confidence.

Leading Starts with Hiring

At first glance, hiring might seem like an odd place to focus when discussing clarity of purpose, leading with vision, and knowing your role as a leader. But here's the truth: hiring is one of the most overlooked yet powerful levers of leadership. Hiring is a process often seen by leaders as a burden, instead of a powerful lever for clarity.

Too many leaders despise hiring and delegate it to recruiting teams, peer panels, or outside talent agencies. While these resources can support the process, great leaders know that hiring is their accountability—and their first real opportunity to lead with clarity of purpose.

The interview process is a critical moment where leaders get to share their vision, articulate the organization's vision, and—most importantly—ask candidates about their own vision. It's not just about filling a role; it's about creating alignment. When a candidate's personal vision connects with the team's purpose and the organization's goals, it lays the groundwork for shared success.

Great leaders understand that their ability to lead effectively depends on the talent they bring onto the team. And talent isn't just about technical skills; it's about cultural alignment, shared values, and the capacity to embrace and contribute to the organization's vision.

Hiring is where leadership begins. It's where you first inspire others with your vision, set the tone for the culture, and establish the alignment that ensures everyone is rowing in the same direction. Leaders who approach hiring with intentionality don't just fill positions—they build teams that thrive.

Enhancing Interviewing Skills: The Foundation of Visionary Leadership

The hiring process isn't just about filling open roles—it's a critical step in building a cohesive, high-performing team. For leaders, this process begins with intentionality and clarity. Every hire should align with the organization's vision, culture, and goals. **Hiring with purpose** sets the stage for effective onboarding, long-term performance management, and team cohesion.

In fact, performance management starts at the interview—where expectations, alignment, and potential are first assessed and cultivated. Interviews are a leader's first opportunity to showcase the organization's vision, share their own, and uncover whether the candidate's vision aligns. The interview process should always remain in the control of the leader. Not always the execution.

The Role of Vision in Hiring

Intentional hiring begins with the leader's own clarity of purpose. A leader who understands the organization's vision and values can clearly articulate these during interviews, framing the role as more than just a job—it's an opportunity to contribute to a shared vision.

Candidates who resonate with this vision are more likely to feel inspired, motivated, and committed from day one. When leaders communicate the "why" behind the role and its connection to organizational goals, they create a sense of purpose that can drive engagement and performance.

Hiring with Onboarding in Mind

A successful hiring process doesn't end when the offer letter is signed—it lays the groundwork for seamless onboarding and long-term integration. Leaders should evaluate not only whether the candidate fits the immediate role but also how they might grow within the organization.

Proactive onboarding starts in the interview. Consider how the candidate's strengths align with the team's goals and how their potential can be nurtured. A clear path from hiring to onboarding ensures new team members are prepared to integrate into the culture and contribute meaningfully to the organization's success.

A great process to include in the interview is sharing the first 90 days plan with candidates. Ask for their input and thoughts: How would they approach the first 90 days? What would they prioritize? How would they define success during that period? Use the onboarding process as a selection tool to gauge their strategic thinking and alignment with the role.

Building Strong Interviewing Skills

To identify candidates who align with the organization's vision and culture, leaders must refine their interviewing skills. This goes beyond checking off technical qualifications—it's about assessing values, cultural alignment, and the candidate's ability to contribute to the team's dynamic.

A Few Key Interviewing Processes

- **Ask Open-Ended Questions**: Prompt candidates to share more than surface-level answers. This reveals their thought process, values, and potential alignment with the organization.
  - Examples:

    - "Can you tell me about a time when you worked in an environment that didn't align with your values? How did you handle it?"
    - "What excites you most about the possibility of joining our team and contributing to our vision?"

- **Listen Actively**: Effective interviewing isn't just about asking questions; it's about truly listening. Pay attention to cues that reveal the candidate's motivations, values, and fit. Practice paraphrasing and summarizing their responses to ensure mutual understanding.
- **Assess for Cultural Fit**: Design questions to evaluate how well the candidate's values align with the team's culture.
  - Examples:
    - "What does teamwork mean to you, and how have you fostered collaboration in previous roles?"
    - "Our culture prioritizes [specific value]. How does that align with how you approach work?"

Note: Cultural fit isn't about hiring people who think the same way—it's about ensuring their values complement the team's dynamics and foster collaboration.

- **Tie the Role to Vision and Purpose**: Share how the role contributes to the organization's larger vision and goals. When candidates see the purpose behind their potential contributions, they are more likely to engage deeply with the role.
  - Example:
    - "This role is key to achieving our vision of [specific goal]. How do you see yourself contributing to that?"

Performance Management Begins at the Interview

Earlier I referred to this concept that perfromance management begins in the interview. Lets unpack this a little more. It might seem odd to bring up performance management while unpacking the importance of clarity of purpose in hiring. But here's the reality: all performance management begins at the interview.

The interview isn't just about evaluating a candidate's skills or filling an open role—it's where the foundation for performance is laid. The clearer and more intentional you are during the hiring process, the less time and energy you'll spend later managing poor performance. In fact, when leaders put the right effort into the interview, they set the stage for long-term success, making "managing" performance less about addressing problems and more about fostering growth.

The seeds of performance management are planted long before a new hire steps into the role—**they're planted during the hiring process.** Leaders who clearly communicate expectations, metrics for success, and opportunities for growth set the foundation for long-term performance. Interviews aren't just about finding the right candidate; they're about laying the groundwork for their success within the organization.

Processes to Connect Interviews to Performance Management

1. Set Clear Expectations

During the interview, outline what success looks like in the role. Be specific about the goals, benchmarks, and deliverables the candidate will be expected to achieve. When expectations are transparent from the start, candidates walk in with clarity and confidence, knowing exactly what's required of them.

Example:

- "In this role, success looks like achieving a 15% increase in client retention over the next six months by implementing new engagement strategies."

2. Discuss Feedback Culture

Explain how feedback is shared and how performance is evaluated within the team. Transparency about the feedback process fosters trust and prepares candidates for a growth-oriented environment. Let them know that feedback isn't punitive—it's a tool for development and success.

Example:

- "We believe in continuous feedback. You'll have biweekly check-ins to discuss progress, roadblocks, and opportunities for growth."

3. Evaluate Potential for Growth

Use the interview to assess the candidate's adaptability and willingness to learn. Ask questions that reveal how they approach challenges, acquire new skills, and navigate unfamiliar territory. This helps identify candidates who align with the organization's growth mindset.

Example:

- "Tell me about a time you had to quickly acquire new skills to succeed in a role. How did you approach it?"

Integrating the Right Talent: From Interview to Onboarding

Hiring the right talent is only the beginning. The next step is onboarding—**a critical phase that ensures new hires integrate into the team and contribute effectively.** Leaders should design onboarding experiences that reinforce the vision, culture, and expectations communicated during the interview.

Onboarding Best Practices

1. Reinforce the Vision

Reiterate the organization's vision and how the new hire's role contributes to it. Help them understand the "why" behind their work to create a sense of purpose from day one.

Example:

- "Our vision is to deliver exceptional customer service. Your role as [position] is essential to achieving that by [specific contribution]."

2. Establish Early Wins

Set achievable goals for the first 30–90 days. Early accomplishments build confidence, demonstrate the new hire's value to the team, and create momentum for future success.

Example:

- "Your first milestone is to streamline our onboarding process for new clients by the end of the first quarter."

3. Connect to Culture

Pair new hires with mentors or buddies who can help them navigate the organization's culture, values, and expectations. These connections foster engagement and accelerate integration.

Interviewing Key Takeaways

- **Vision and Process-Centered Hiring:** Ensure candidates align with the organization's vision, values, and goals during the hiring process. Use a formal process. Do not wing it.
- **Cultural Fit Matters:** Assess candidates for alignment with the team's culture and dynamics, not just technical skills.
- **Performance Management Starts Early:** Use the interview to establish clear expectations, goals, and opportunities for growth.

- **Onboarding is an Extension of Hiring:** Reinforce vision and culture in the first 90 days to ensure successful integration.

Great leaders understand that building a high-performing team begins long before the first day on the job. **Intentionality in the hiring process ensures that every new team member is not only equipped for the role but also aligned with the organization's vision and culture.**

By connecting the dots between hiring, onboarding, and performance management, leaders create a seamless experience that sets their teams —and themselves—up for long-term success. Through thoughtful interviewing, leaders demonstrate the values and purpose they wish to see in their teams, laying the foundation for a culture of clarity, collaboration, and achievement.

Chapter 1: Key Takeaways

- **Clarity is Foundational**: Effective leadership begins with a clear understanding of the organization's vision, vision, and values, which must be communicated consistently to align the team's efforts. Know your "why" and share it often.

- **Leaders as Visionaries**: Leaders are responsible for creating, articulating, and embedding the organizational vision into daily operations to inspire and guide their teams.

- **Distinct Roles**: Leadership is about strategic oversight and fostering team alignment, while individual contributors focus on executing specific tasks that support the broader vision.

- **Transitioning to Leadership**: Moving from an individual contributor role to a leadership position requires shifting from personal task execution to guiding team dynamics and aligning efforts with organizational objectives.

- **Building Culture Through Vision**: Effective leaders connect their personal and professional vision to the organization's vision, creating authenticity and inspiring team alignment.
- **Fostering an Asking Culture**: Leaders should consistently engage with their team members to understand their aspirations, aligning personal goals with organizational objectives to foster connection and motivation.
- **Common Leadership Mistakes**: Avoid pitfalls such as failing to delegate, neglecting personal growth, and avoiding difficult conversations by employing proactive strategies like setting clear goals, seeking feedback, and empowering team members.
- **Intentional Hiring Practices**: Performance management begins in the interview process. Leaders must assess candidates for cultural fit, alignment with vision, and potential for growth.
- **Onboarding Sets the Tone**: An intentional onboarding process reinforces the organization's vision and values, establishing early wins and integrating new hires effectively into the team.
- **Leadership with Clarity is a Process**: Leading with clarity of purpose is an ongoing journey of intentionality, reflection, and consistent reinforcement of vision and culture.

By understanding and applying these principles, leaders can create a clear path for themselves and their teams, leading to greater alignment, effectiveness, and satisfaction in their roles.

Processes for Implementation

1. **Develop and Communicate Your "Why"**

- **Reflect on Your Vision:** Take time to articulate why you lead and how your personal goals align with the organization's vision.

- **Share Your Purpose:** Regularly communicate your "why" with your team, weaving it into meetings, one-on-ones, and everyday conversations.

2. **Align Personal and Organizational Goals**

- **Bridge the Gap:** Ensure your personal purpose is aligned with the broader organizational vision.

- **Help Your Team Find Alignment:** Engage team members in discussions about how their roles contribute to the bigger picture and how their individual goals connect with the organization's vision.

3. **Cultivate an "Asking" Culture**

- **Ask the Right Questions:** Encourage team members to share their aspirations, motivations, and values.

- **Foster Openness:** Create an environment where dialogue is encouraged, and people feel safe discussing their personal "why."

4. **Set Clear Expectations and Roles**

- **Define Success:** Clearly outline each team member's responsibilities and how their contributions align with the organization's goals.

- **Provide Feedback:** Establish regular feedback loops to ensure alignment and address any gaps between expectations and performance.

5. **Invest in Hiring with Clarity**

- **Vision-Driven Interviews:** Use the interview process to share the organization's vision and assess candidates for alignment.

- **Set the Stage for Success:** Lay the groundwork for performance management during hiring by clearly communicating expectations and goals.

6. **Delegate with Confidence**

- **Focus on Leadership:** Avoid slipping back into individual contributor mode; delegate tasks and focus on creating the conditions for team success.
- **Empower Your Team:** Trust your team to handle their responsibilities and provide them with the tools and support they need to succeed.

Chapter 2
SETTING DIRECTION

"If you don't know where you're going, you'll end up someplace else."
— Yogi Berra

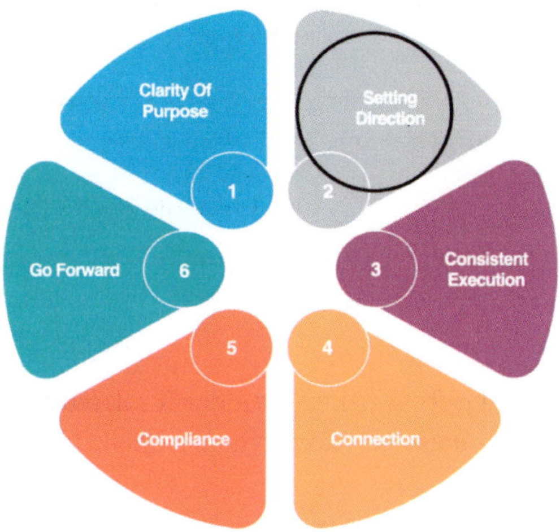

"You hit only what you aim at." This simple yet profound principle underscores the essence of *Leading by Design*: without clear direction, even the most talented teams will struggle to achieve meaningful outcomes. **Setting Direction** isn't just about outlining tasks or creating to-do lists—it's about providing a roadmap that inspires, aligns, and empowers a team to move with purpose toward a shared vision. This is the next category or component to the model. With a clear purpose in hand, we can now set direction.

Vision and purpose without direction is like a GPS without a destination—sure, you're moving, but are you getting anywhere? Setting Direction is where leaders step up to create clarity in the chaos, mapping the path forward and rallying their teams to move with intent. This isn't about micromanaging tasks; it's about crafting a the map to a vision so compelling that your team is energized and focused to achieve it. A well-directed team is a high-performing team, and unlocking that performance lies in your ability to **align, communicate, and execute**.

Vision In Pieces

Having a vision is meaningless if you can't communicate it effectively. You could draft the most brilliant vision for the world, but if your team doesn't understand it, believe in it, or care about it, it's dead on arrival. I've lost count of the number of company lobbies and boardrooms I've walked into with vision statements beautifully displayed on the walls. Yet, most employees can't tell you what those words mean, let alone how they're working toward achieving them.

That's not just a missed opportunity—that's a failure of leadership. Employees might know what's written in their performance plans, but that's usually the extent of their understanding. Don't believe me? Try this: walk around your organization and ask, **"What is the company vision?" or "What's our roadmap for getting there?"** Chances are, you'll encounter a lot of blank stares or vague responses. And those that do know it, most likely do not know the pieces of how they will get there. Most people just know a job description and their annual performance plan.

Communicating direction isn't just about sharing a plan; it's about selling the why in clear, actionable pieces. It's about answering two fundamental questions: **Where are we going? and How will we get**

there? If you can't articulate that for your team, don't expect them to follow you. Leadership demands clarity and connection, and those start with effective communication.

Effective leaders paint a vivid picture of what success looks like and why it matters through the smaller pieces that relate through the organization. They create alignment by connecting the team's daily efforts to the broader vision. When people see how their work contributes to something larger than themselves, they don't just follow orders—they **buy in. Goals are the "how" you communicate vision deep into an organization.**

Making Communication a Two-Way Street

Here's the kicker: communication is a **two-way street.** If you're only telling and never listening, you're missing the mark. Great leaders engage their teams in shaping the direction. They involve their teams in answering the critical question: ***how will we get there?*** Goal setting is a chance to engage and pull in your teams into the direction.

Involving your team in the process isn't a sign of weakness; it's a demonstration of strength. Inviting input, fielding questions, and creating a space where everyone feels invested in the outcome fosters trust, collaboration, and motivation. When people feel heard, they're more likely to follow you—not because they have to, but because they **want to.**

Turning Vision into Action

Communicating direction isn't just a speech or a PowerPoint slide—it's an ongoing conversation. It's about consistently tying the team's work back to the larger vision, ensuring alignment, and maintaining momentum.

By setting direction collaboratively, leaders not only provide clarity but also empower their teams to contribute to the journey. When everyone understands the **why** and feels part of shaping the **how**, the result is a team that doesn't just execute—they excel.

The Art of Mapping the Path Forward

At its core, setting direction begins with asking two fundamental questions:

1. **Where are we going?**
2. **How will we get there?**

The first question establishes your the details of your vision; the second defines your strategy. Without both, leadership devolves into aimless activity—lots of motion, little progress. Effective leaders define not just the destination but also the roadmap, ensuring every step along the way moves the team closer to its goals.

A strong direction isn't vague or abstract. "Increase sales" isn't a direction; it's an aspiration. "Increase Q1 sales by 15% by launching a targeted marketing campaign and doubling our outbound calls" is a direction. The difference? **Specificity, focus, and actionability.** As a leader, your job is to translate big-picture vision into tangible steps your team can execute.

The Power of Clear Objectives

Here's the secret sauce: **clear objectives are the currency of great leadership.** A goal that isn't specific is a goal that won't be achieved. When your team knows exactly what success looks like—and how to measure it—they move with clarity and confidence.

This is why the **SMART framework** (Specific, Measurable, Achievable, Relevant, Time-bound) isn't just management jargon; it's a necessity.

Consider this: "Let's improve customer satisfaction" sounds nice, but what does it actually mean? How will you measure it? Who is responsible for it? What's the timeline? Throughout this section you will hear the theme **"What gets measured, gets done."** Without goals, you cannot measure. Leadership is about taking lofty aspirations and breaking them into achievable chunks. You're not just pointing to the mountaintop; you're plotting the trail to get there.

Where Strategy Meets Execution

Daily leadership lives at the intersection of **strategy and execution.** It's not enough to have a vision; you need a plan to achieve it. And it's not enough to have a plan; you need the discipline to see it through.

This component of the **Leading by Design Model**, equips leaders with the tools to define goals, communicate them effectively, and manage tasks and relationships with precision. It's where the theoretical meets the practical, where big ideas get turned into big results.

Here's what great leaders do in this space:

- **Set the North Star:** Define a compelling vision that aligns with the organization's vision.
- **Break It Down:** Turn that vision into specific, measurable objectives.
- **Get Buy-In:** Communicate the plan with clarity and engage the team in its execution.
- **Remove Barriers:** Identify and eliminate obstacles that slow progress.
- **Track Progress:** Use tools and metrics to monitor execution and adjust the course as needed.

Why It Matters

Without direction, teams flounder. They waste time, energy, and resources chasing unclear goals or, worse, working at cross-purposes. But with clear direction, teams thrive. They move with **intention, focus, and cohesion.**

As a leader, your ability to set direction is what separates you from the pack. It's not just about having a vision—it's about turning that vision into reality. It's where strategy meets execution, where leadership becomes more than an idea and transforms into action. And when done right, it's the difference between a team that merely works and a team that **wins.**

Defining SMART Goals and Metrics

This is the **"how"** we set direction. **SMART goals—Specific, Measurable, Achievable, Relevant, and Time-bound—**are a proven framework for creating objectives that actually work. This approach ensures that goals are not only clear and actionable but also aligned with the team's overarching vision and vision. By adopting SMART goals, leaders can provide their teams with direction, focus, and motivation while fostering accountability and continuous improvement.

SMART goals don't just give your team clarity—they make success tangible. When paired with metrics, they offer a concrete way to track progress, celebrate milestones, and make informed adjustments. The combination of SMART goals and metrics transforms abstract ambitions into a roadmap for achievement.

Here's the surprising part: every time I teach **Leading by Design**, I ask the room, "How many of you know what SMART goals are?" Almost always, at least half the hands go up. Then I follow with, "How many of you actually use them?" That's when nearly every hand drops—leaving one or two at most. When I ask why they don't use them, the answers are almost always the same: **"I feel like goals are a judgment of my performance,"** or **"I just don't see the value."**

It's time to change that. Here's how:

1. **Let go of the fear of judgment.** Goals aren't about proving your worth; they're about defining success on your terms as a leader. When you take ownership of that definition, goals become tools—not threats.

2. **Embrace the process.** With the **Leading by Design** framework, you now have an entire process from start to finish. SMART goals are no longer just another task on your to-do list; they're the glue

that ties the model together. When implemented with intention, they create alignment and empower your team to see the value and purpose behind their work.

Let's move past the excuses and start setting SMART goals that inspire action, enable growth, and drive results—not just for your team but for your leadership. Because at the end of the day, success isn't something that happens to you; it's something you design.

Why SMART Goals Matter

SMART goals empower teams to move with clarity and confidence. By defining precise objectives and measurable outcomes, leaders ensure that their teams are not only working hard but also working smart—focusing efforts on what truly matters. With SMART goals and metrics in place, leaders can lead their teams with precision, continually assessing progress and making informed decisions to drive results.

Two major truths I've learned underscore the importance of effective goal setting. The first is, ***"What gets measured gets done."*** I told you we would hair on this one. Goals without metrics are like targets in the dark—impossible to hit with any consistency. Measurement brings focus, accountability, and clarity, ensuring that efforts are directed where they matter most. The second truth is one I hold dearly as a leader: ***"In God I trust; all others better bring data."*** While faith and instinct play a role in leadership, decisions must be grounded in tangible evidence. Data provides the clarity and objectivity needed to evaluate progress, identify challenges, and make informed adjustments. I have seen so many leaders fail and teams fall into dysfunction, simply because they work on feelings and assumptions instead of juts using and pinning to dat to make decisions, recover from failures, and find when to celebrate. Together, these truths reinforce that clear goals, paired with measurable outcomes, are essential tools for any leader aiming to inspire action and achieve meaningful results.

Breaking Down the SMART Framework

1. Specific:

A goal must be clear and detailed, leaving no room for ambiguity. Vague goals can lead to confusion and lack of focus. Instead, a specific goal provides team members with a precise understanding of what is expected.

Example:

- Regular Goal: "Increase sales."
- SMART Goal: "Increase product sales in the Southeast region by 15% within the next quarter."

2. Measurable:

Goals must include quantifiable criteria to track progress and determine when they have been achieved. Without measurement, it's difficult to know if a goal is on track or complete.

Example:

- Regular Goal: "Improve customer satisfaction."
- SMART Goal: "Achieve a 10% increase in customer satisfaction scores, as measured by post-service surveys, by the end of the next quarter."

3. Achievable:

Goals should be challenging but realistic. Overly ambitious goals can lead to frustration and burnout, while easily attainable goals fail to inspire growth. Leaders must consider available resources, constraints, and team capabilities when defining what's achievable.

Example:

- Regular Goal: "Launch a new product line."

- SMART Goal: "Launch the new eco-friendly product line in three major markets by the end of the fiscal year, with a dedicated marketing budget of $50,000."

4. Relevant:

Goals need to align with the broader objectives of the organization. A relevant goal connects to the team's mission and priorities, ensuring that efforts contribute meaningfully to overall success.

Example:

- Regular Goal: "Reduce costs."
- SMART Goal: "Reduce supply chain costs by 10% over the next six months by renegotiating vendor contracts, supporting our overall profitability targets."

5. Time-bound:

Every goal needs a deadline to create urgency and enable effective prioritization. Deadlines encourage team members to manage their time and resources wisely to meet expectations.

Example:

- Regular Goal: "Enhance employee training programs."
- SMART Goal: "Develop and implement a new employee training program for onboarding within 60 days, and ensure 90% of new hires complete the program within their first month."

Transforming Non-SMART Goals Into SMART Goals

Here are examples of how to convert vague goals into SMART ones:

Non-SMART Goal #1: "Grow the team's social media presence."

SMART Goal: "Increase the team's LinkedIn followers by 20% over the next 90 days through weekly content posting and engagement campaigns."

Non-SMART Goal #2: "Enhance workplace collaboration."

SMART Goal: "Implement a new project management tool within 30 days, and ensure 100% of team members are trained to use it effectively within two weeks of implementation."

Non-SMART Goal #3: "Improve product quality."

SMART Goal: "Decrease the defect rate in the manufacturing process by 15% within the next six months through updated training and equipment calibration."

Metrics: The Key to Measuring Success

Metrics play a crucial role in the effectiveness of SMART goals by providing tangible benchmarks for progress. They answer the question: How will we know when we've succeeded? Metrics enable leaders to:

- **Track Progress**: Regularly monitor milestones to ensure the team stays on track.
- **Adjust Strategies**: Use data to identify areas where adjustments are needed to meet goals.
- **Celebrate Success**: Highlight achievements with measurable evidence of progress.

For example, if the SMART goal is to "Increase customer retention rates by 5% within six months," relevant metrics might include the number of repeat purchases, renewal rates, or customer satisfaction scores.

SMART goals are more than a framework—they're the compass that keeps leaders and their teams on course. By anchoring efforts in clear, measurable, and relevant objectives, leaders empower their teams to focus on what truly matters. This isn't about endless busywork; it's about purposeful action that drives real results.

The power of SMART goals lies in their ability to transform ambiguity into clarity and potential into performance. They give leaders the tools to not only set direction but to track progress, adapt when needed, and celebrate achievements along the way. When paired with metrics, SMART goals create a culture of accountability and transparency, where success is not just a hope but an expectation.

As you reflect on how to apply SMART goals, ask yourself: What does success look like for you and your team? How can you measure it? And most importantly, how can you lead with the clarity and confidence that SMART goals provide? Remember, leadership isn't about perfection—it's about progress. And progress starts with a well-defined target.

Making Goals Heard and Understood

Communication is the backbone of effective leadership, as we have visited earlier in small short bursts, especially when it comes to setting and achieving goals. A leader may have a clear vision and well-defined objectives, but without effective communication, those goals remain unrealized. The truth is, many goals fail not because they are unachievable but because they are not adequately communicated. Communicating goals is not just about telling people what needs to be done—it's about ensuring that everyone understands the purpose, priorities, and their role in achieving success.

Why Communicating Goals Is Essential

1. **Clarity Drives Action**: Goals that are not clearly communicated leave room for assumptions and misunderstandings. When team members don't fully understand the objectives or their responsibilities, they may focus their efforts in the wrong direction. Clear communication bridges this gap, ensuring alignment and focus across the team.

2. **Creates Buy-In**: Effective communication involves more than delivering instructions—it's about inspiring and engaging the team. When leaders take the time to explain the "why" behind a goal and how it connects to the broader vision, it fosters a sense of ownership and motivation among team members.

3. **Ensures Accountability**: Goals that are shared and understood provide a framework for accountability. When everyone knows the expectations, timelines, and metrics for success, it becomes easier to track progress and hold each other accountable.

4. **Builds Trust and Collaboration**: Transparent communication about goals shows that leaders trust their teams and value their input. It encourages open dialogue, collaboration, and a shared commitment to achieving success.

How to Effectively Communicate Goals

1. Use Multiple Channels

Communication is most effective when it reaches people in ways they best understand. Share goals in team meetings, through written documents, visual dashboards, or one-on-one conversations. Repetition across different channels ensures the message is understood and remembered.

Example: Present quarterly goals during a team meeting with a slide deck, then follow up with a detailed email summarizing key points. Use a project management tool to track progress and keep goals visible throughout the quarter.

2. Make the Purpose Clear

Explaining the "why" behind a goal is critical. Connect the goal to the organization's vision or broader objectives. Show how achieving the goal benefits the team, the company, and even individual contributors.

Example: Instead of simply saying, "We need to reduce customer complaints by 15%," explain, "Reducing complaints helps us improve customer retention and builds our reputation as a trusted brand, which supports long-term growth and stability for all of us."

3. Encourage Two-Way Communication

Effective communication is not a one-way street. After sharing goals, create opportunities for questions, feedback, and discussion. Encourage team members to voice their perspectives, ask for clarification, or suggest improvements.

Example: During goal-setting meetings, allocate time for a Q&A session or ask team members to share how they see their roles contributing to the goal. This not only clarifies understanding but also fosters engagement.

4. Break Goals into Actionable Steps

Large goals can feel overwhelming if they're not broken into manageable tasks. Communicate both the big picture and the smaller steps needed to achieve it. This provides clarity on how each team member's work contributes to the overall goal.

Example: If the goal is to "Launch a new product by the end of Q2," break it down into milestones such as completing product design, running a marketing campaign, and preparing for distribution. Assign specific tasks and deadlines to relevant team members.

5. Reinforce Goals Regularly

Communicating a goal once is not enough. Regularly revisit and reinforce goals to keep them top of mind. Provide updates on progress, celebrate milestones, and adjust priorities as needed.

Example: During weekly team meetings, include a brief update on progress toward goals and highlight any achievements. Use this time to re-align efforts or address challenges.

6. Tailor Communication to Your Audience

Recognize that different team members may require different levels of detail or communication styles to fully grasp the goals. Adapt your message to fit their needs and preferences.

Example: While senior managers might appreciate high-level strategic updates, frontline employees may need practical instructions and clear expectations for their specific tasks.

7. Leverage Visual Tools

Visual aids like dashboards, charts, and infographics can make goals more tangible and easier to understand. They provide a clear reference point for tracking progress and maintaining focus.

Example: Use a visual project tracker to display the status of each goal and its associated tasks. This creates transparency and helps the team see how their work contributes to the larger objectives.

Ensure Nothing Falls Through the Cracks

I've seen it far too often: exceptional leaders who crush it when crafting a vision and setting direction but completely drop the ball when it's time to track and measure progress. They pour their energy into the big picture, captivating their teams with ambitious goals and inspiring roadmaps, only to let execution slip through the cracks. Why? Because the day-to-day grind takes over. Endless firefighting, back-to-back meetings, and reactive problem-solving become the focus of a leader's time and attention, leaving no bandwidth for managing the systems that turn vision into reality.

This isn't just an oversight—it's a leadership failure. Great ideas are worthless without the discipline to execute them. **What gets measured gets done.** Without clear systems for project tracking and management, even the most brilliant strategy will collapse under the weight of missed deadlines, unclear responsibilities, and a lack of accountability. You may think this topic should be under the consistent execution part of the Leading by Design Model, but I have found that matching the tool and process at time of setting direction must come before the focus on consistent execution.

Tracking progress isn't just a logistical task—it's an act of leadership. It's how you keep your team aligned, motivated, and moving forward. When leaders neglect this crucial piece, they not only risk underperformance but also erode trust and engagement. Your team starts to wonder: If our leader doesn't care enough to track our progress, why should we?

The truth is, execution doesn't happen by chance. You cannot begin to think about executing, unless you have the proper set up in place. It happens by design. Leaders who prioritize effective tracking and measurement create a culture of accountability where the small wins build momentum and big goals are actually achieved. Let's explore how you can move from inspiring ideas to disciplined follow-through, ensuring your vision doesn't just stay on the whiteboard—it becomes a reality.

The Importance of Project Management

Project management isn't about micromanaging—it's about creating a system that ensures progress is visible, problems are addressed early, and everyone stays aligned with the broader vision. It's the glue that holds the vision and execution together.

- **Clear Visibility:** Effective project management gives leaders and teams a real-time view of where things stand. It highlights what's on track, what's lagging, and where adjustments are needed.
- **Ownership and Accountability:** Assigning clear responsibilities ensures that every task has a designated owner and nothing gets overlooked.
- **Adaptability:** When priorities shift or challenges arise, project tracking allows leaders to pivot quickly without losing momentum.

Tools Aren't Optional

You may be thinking, as I often hear, "What tool should I choose?" Well, choose the one you and the team will actually use. Then I get asked, "Which one is that?" and my answer is always the same: "**Just pick one.**" Stick with it until it no longer serves your needs. You have to commit to a tool and use it consistently long enough for processes to create behaviors, for those behaviors to become habits, and for those habits to impact culture and performance.

Trying to manage complex projects with sticky notes or scattered spreadsheets is a recipe for disaster. The right tools aren't just nice to have—they're essential for keeping everything on track, driving accountability, and ensuring success.

- **Implement Project Management Software:** Platforms like Asana, Trello, or Monday.com aren't just trendy—they're powerful tools to organize tasks, set deadlines, and assign responsibilities. They provide a centralized hub where everyone can see what needs to be done and by when.
- **Automate Where Possible:** Use automation features for reminders, recurring tasks, and updates to save time and reduce human error.
- **Czar it Up:** Pick someone on your team to own the goal tracking. I so often see leaders try to do it all. Gove the reigns go tracking over tot the team. Pick a Goal Czar on your team.

The Power of Regular Updates

Project management tools are great, but they're not a replacement for human interaction. **Regular check-ins** are where the magic happens.

- **Weekly Progress Meetings:** Keep them short and focused. What's done? What's in progress? What's stuck? These sessions ensure everyone stays aligned and gives the team a chance to raise red flags before they become full-blown crises.

- **Celebrate Wins:** Use updates not just to fix issues but to acknowledge progress. Positive momentum is a powerful motivator.

Clear Documentation is Non-Negotiable

Ambiguity kills progress. If no one remembers the decision made in last week's meeting, how can they act on it? Clear documentation eliminates confusion and keeps the team aligned.

- **Decisions in Writing:** Capture all key decisions in writing and share them with the team. This avoids miscommunication and provides a single source of truth.
- **Change Tracking:** When plans shift—and they will—ensure changes are documented and communicated to everyone involved.

Why It Matters

Vision without setting direction is hallucination. Leaders who talk vision and fail to set a direction and follow through risk losing credibility and momentum. By prioritizing project management and tracking, you bridge the gap between ambition and action.

When you make tracking progress a non-negotiable part of leadership, you ensure that nothing falls through the cracks, no effort is wasted, and every step moves the team closer to the goal. Because at the end of the day, **what gets measured gets done.**

Managing Relationships Up and Across

I almost always get funny looks when I get to the topic in the model. Setting direction isn't just about rallying your own team; it's about ensuring alignment across the organization. Leaders must manage relationships not only with their team but also with their superiors and peers to create a cohesive and unified path forward.

Here's the reality: **direction-setting doesn't happen in a vacuum.** Even if you've nailed the vision for your team, your efforts can stall if they conflict with the goals of other departments or fail to gain buy-in from leadership. To truly set direction effectively, you need alignment both **up** and **across** the organization.

Balancing Tasks and Relationships

Setting direction isn't just about managing tasks—it's about managing relationships. A leader who focuses solely on the work risks losing sight of the people doing it. The best leaders know that execution relies on **trust, collaboration, and motivation.** It's not enough to delegate tasks; you need to ensure the team has the support and resources they need to succeed.

Relationships are your leadership equity. If your team trusts you, they'll follow you through uncertainty, setbacks, and change. Without that trust, even the most well-laid plans will falter. Setting direction, then, isn't just about handing out marching orders—it's about building the relational foundation that ensures those orders are carried out with commitment and enthusiasm.

Managing Up: Gaining Buy-In from Leadership

Leaders often focus so much on their teams that they forget the importance of managing relationships with their superiors. Setting direction requires **ensuring those above you in the hierarchy are aligned with your vision and supportive of your team's initiatives.**

- **Communicate the "Why" and the "How":** When presenting your direction to upper management, emphasize how it aligns with the broader organizational goals. Show them how your strategy supports the company's vision, addresses key priorities, or solves critical challenges.
- **Preempt Resistance:** Understand potential concerns or objections leadership might have and address them proactively. This shows you've thought through your direction holistically.
- **Advocate for Resources:** Make a compelling case for the tools, funding, or headcount your team needs to execute effectively.

Leadership can't support what they don't understand, so be clear and specific about what's required and why.

- **Keep Leadership Informed:** Regularly update your superiors on progress, challenges, and wins. This builds trust and ensures they remain invested in your direction.

Managing Across: Collaborating with Peers

Setting direction also means **working horizontally across the organization** to ensure alignment with other departments and stakeholders. Just because you've set a clear path for your team doesn't mean it exists in isolation. The success of your vision often hinges on how well it aligns with the directions set by your peers in other areas of the organization.

- **Understand Others' Goals:** Take the time to learn what drives other departments. What are their priorities? What challenges are they addressing? This understanding helps identify areas where your directions overlap or conflict.
- **Build Alliances:** Collaboration isn't just helpful—it's essential. Develop relationships with peers that foster smoother cooperation and resource sharing. These alliances make it easier to navigate interdependencies and reduce friction between teams.
- **Seek Alignment:** Proactively engage with other stakeholders to align strategies. If you're in operations, make sure you understand what business development, marketing, or finance is doing. This prevents duplication of effort or competing priorities.

Advocacy and Negotiation

Whether managing up or across, leaders must also become skilled advocates and negotiators. Setting direction requires **making the case for your team's needs and contributions** while ensuring they align with organizational priorities.

- **Advocate for Your Team:** Clearly communicate how your team's work contributes to organizational success. Highlight achievements and make it clear why your team's initiatives deserve support.
- **Negotiate Resources:** In a world of finite resources, negotiation is inevitable. Work collaboratively to secure the tools, funding, or personnel your team needs, while respecting the needs of other departments.
- **Create Win-Win Scenarios:** Look for opportunities where alignment benefits everyone. For example, aligning your direction with business development's goals might create efficiencies that enhance results for both teams.

Why It Matters

Leadership isn't just about managing down; it's about creating alignment across the entire organization. Without buy-in from leadership, your direction lacks the support and resources needed to succeed. Without collaboration with peers, your efforts risk being siloed or counterproductive.

By managing up and across effectively, you ensure that your team's direction is part of a larger, cohesive strategy. This creates alignment, reduces friction, and ensures everyone is rowing in the same direction —toward success.

Chapter 2 Key Takeaways

1. **SMART Goals:**

Setting goals isn't just about having something to aim for—it's about creating a clear path to success. Use the **SMART framework** (Specific, Measurable, Achievable, Relevant, Time-bound) to establish objectives that are actionable and directly aligned with your organization's strategic priorities. Goals that lack specificity or measurability often lead to confusion and wasted effort.

2. Communication Excellence:

Great direction means nothing without great communication. Develop and refine your communication skills by emphasizing **clarity, active listening, and effective feedback.** Ensure your team not only understands the vision but feels invested in it. Remember, communication is a two-way street—listening is just as important as speaking.

3. Efficient Project Tracking:

Vision without execution is hallucination. Leverage **project management tools and techniques** to ensure that tasks stay on track, deadlines are met, and accountability is maintained. Use regular check-ins, clear documentation, and progress metrics to keep your team aligned and focused. **What gets measured gets done.**

4. Relationship Management:

Direction doesn't happen in a silo. Foster strong relationships with both your superiors and peers to build alignment and secure support for your team's initiatives. Take the time to understand the goals of other departments, advocate for your team's needs, and negotiate resources. Leadership isn't just about managing down—it's about creating cohesion across the organization.

Processes for Implementation

1. Goal-Setting Workshops:

Educate your team on the power of **SMART goals** by conducting interactive workshops. These sessions should focus on helping team members understand how to set clear, measurable objectives and align them with the organization's strategic priorities. Use real-world examples and hands-on exercises to ensure participants leave with actionable goals they can immediately implement.

2. Communication Training Sessions:

Great communication doesn't happen by accident—it's a skill that requires continuous development. Implement regular training sessions that focus on key areas like **clarity, active listening, providing feedback, and managing difficult conversations.** Consider using role-playing scenarios to make these sessions engaging and practical, allowing team members to apply new techniques in real-time.

3. Monthly Review Meetings:

Schedule **monthly strategy meetings** to keep your team aligned and focused. Use these meetings to review project progress, celebrate milestones, and discuss challenges. Dedicate time to adjust goals or priorities as needed based on current progress and organizational shifts. Consistency is key—these meetings should become a reliable space for alignment, accountability, and problem-solving.

4. Cross-Departmental Meetings:

Silos kill momentum. Initiate regular meetings with other departments to foster collaboration, enhance communication, and ensure alignment of goals and strategies across the organization. These meetings should focus on identifying interdependencies, resolving conflicts, and uncovering opportunities for shared success. Building relationships across departments ensures your team's direction supports broader organizational objectives.

By mastering the art of setting direction, leaders can ensure their teams are focused, motivated, and aligned with the organization's broader objectives, leading to enhanced performance and success.

Chapter 3

CONSISTENT EXECUTION

"Amateurs sit and wait for inspiration,
the rest of us just get up and go to work."
– Stephen King

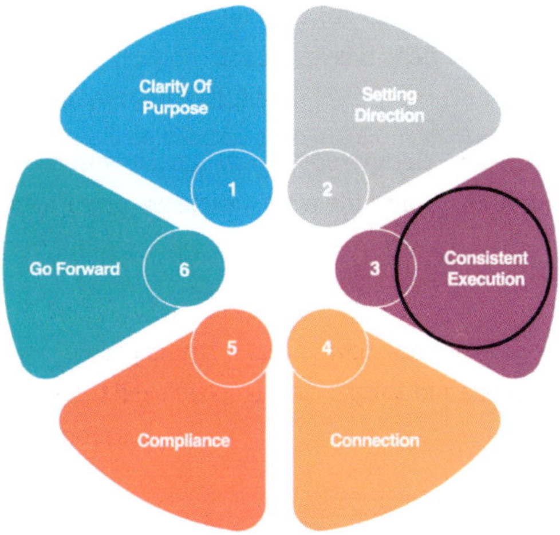

Consistent Execution is the boring weapon of world domination. It's not glamorous, but it's what separates leaders who inspire for a moment from those who build legacies. Great ideas, charismatic speeches, and big visions might get you attention, but consistent execution is what turns those ideas into results and that attention into influence.

Leadership isn't just about standing in the spotlight delivering inspiring speeches or brainstorming brilliant ideas on a whiteboard. Then pointing a direction and saying, "let me know how it goes." Those moments are great, but they're not what measures true leadership. **Leadership is showing up every day**—on the tough days, the chaotic days, and the days when no one's watching. It's about the grind, the follow-through, and the unrelenting discipline to turn vision into reality.

If a consistent execution was someone in the army it takes to pull off a rock concert, it wouldn't be the glamorous lead singer basking in the spotlight—it would be the roadie hauling gear backstage. Unseen, uncelebrated, but utterly essential. Without it, the show doesn't go on.

Consistent execution is where vision and goals meets reality. It's where the rubber hits the road, where ideas transform into results, and where leaders earn their stripes. **Consistent execution isn't just a virtue; it's a radical pursuit.**

Let's break down what **consistent execution** really means within the **Leading by Design** model. It doesn't mean the leader gets up every day and does the work for the team. In fact, slipping back into the role of a subject matter expert or star individual contributor—the very skills that may have propelled you into leadership—undermines your ability to lead effectively.

Consistent execution as a leader is about creating the right conditions for your team to succeed. It's about ensuring they have the environment, tools, and resources necessary to achieve their goals. Leadership isn't about doing the work; it's about equipping your team to do the work better than you ever could.

Why Consistency Matters

Leadership isn't measured by good intentions; it's measured by outcomes. No one cares how visionary your plans are if they never materialize. Consistent execution ensures that your efforts lead to tangible, measurable results.

Teams don't follow leaders who are brilliant one day and absent the next. They follow leaders who show up, follow through, and make things happen. **Consistency breeds reliability, and reliability builds trust.**

And trust? That's your leadership currency. When you consistently deliver results, your team knows they can count on you. That trust isn't just a bonus—it's what empowers you to inspire, influence, and motivate your team to perform at their best. Without trust, your leadership crumbles, no matter how grand your vision may be.

Creating the Environment for Success

Consistent execution starts with the leader's responsibility to set the stage. This means:

- **Defining and Redefining clear goals:** Your team needs to understand what success looks like and how their efforts contribute to it. And adjusting along the way.
- **Providing the right resources:** From training to technology, leaders must ensure their teams have the tools they need to deliver.
- **Removing obstacles:** Identify and eliminate barriers that slow progress, whether they're bottlenecks in processes, unclear priorities, or external distractions.
- **Maintaining alignment:** Regularly check in to ensure everyone remains focused on the team's priorities and aligned with the organization's vision.

But creating the right environment goes beyond logistics and strategy —it requires **prioritization, time management, delegation, and the discipline to say no. And guess what, they are all processes:**

- **Prioritization:** Help your team focus on what truly matters by setting clear priorities and cutting through the noise of competing demands.
- **Time Management:** Teach your team to manage their time effectively by modeling best practices like time-blocking and aligning tasks with peak energy hours.
- **Delegation:** Empower your team by assigning responsibilities that match their strengths and give them the autonomy to succeed. Delegation isn't just a time-saver—it's a trust-builder.
- **Saying No:** Protect your team's focus and energy by learning to say no to low-priority tasks or initiatives that don't align with the bigger vision. Saying no strategically ensures that resources are directed where they'll have the most impact.

Great leaders don't just hand out tasks—they create an environment where those tasks can be executed efficiently and effectively. Your job is to make sure the path is clear, the priorities are sharp, and the team is equipped to walk it.

In this chapter, we'll break down four critical pillars of consistent execution: prioritization, time management, delegation, and the superpower of saying "no."

Prioritization: Not all tasks are created equal, and trying to do everything at once is a recipe for overwhelm. We'll explore how to cut through the noise, focus on what truly matters, and make impactful decisions using tools like the Eisenhower Matrix.

Time Management: Every leader has the same 24 hours, but the way you manage your time can set you apart. From time-blocking to aligning tasks with your peak energy, we'll dive into strategies to maximize focus and productivity.

Delegation: You can't (and shouldn't) do it all yourself. Delegation isn't just about handing off tasks—it's about scaling your impact, empowering your team, and building trust. We'll discuss how to delegate effectively and avoid common pitfalls.

The Superpower of Saying "No": Leaders are constantly bombarded with requests, and while saying yes feels like the right move, it often spreads you too thin. Learning to say no strategically is a game-changer that protects your focus and keeps your priorities intact.

By mastering these four areas, you'll build a foundation of consistent execution that drives results, fosters trust, and sets the tone for your team to follow. Leadership isn't about perfection—it's about showing up and delivering every single day. Let's get into it.

Busy Is Not Productive

Let's get something out in the open: **busy is NOT productive.** In fact, the word "busy" is one of the most dangerous red flags in a team environment. Whenever I'm invited to observe teams, one of the first things I look for is how often I hear people say, **"I'm so busy."**

Here's why that matters: **busy** doesn't mean progress. It doesn't mean goals are being met or problems are being solved. What it does mean is that the environment the leader has set up isn't one built for consistent execution. Instead, it's an environment filled with:

- **Unintentional work:** Tasks that don't move the needle but fill time.
- **A lack of prioritization:** Energy spent on what's loudest, not what's most impactful.
- **Minimal delegation:** Leaders or team members hoarding responsibilities instead of empowering others.
- **Reaction over proactivity:** Reward systems that celebrate quick responses to crises instead of thoughtful, strategic planning.

The Difference Between Busy and Productive

The difference between busy and productive isn't subtle—it's monumental. Busy people are reactive; productive people are proactive. Busy teams spend their days putting out fires, chasing every email, and attending back-to-back meetings that lead nowhere. Productive teams, on the other hand, align their efforts with clear goals, measure their progress, and focus on what matters most.

Here's how to distinguish the two:

- **Busy:** Feels chaotic, scattered, and rushed. It's about looking active, not achieving results.
- **Productive:** Feels intentional, focused, and deliberate. It's about making meaningful progress toward defined objectives.

Busy teams often equate effort with value—if they're working hard, they must be doing well. But hard work without direction is just wasted energy. Productive teams, however, understand that value comes from outcomes, not effort.

The Case to Eradicate the Word "Busy"

If you want to create an environment of consistent execution, it's time to banish the word "busy" from your team's vocabulary. Here's why:

1. **"Busy" is vague:** It communicates nothing about priorities or progress.
2. **"Busy" is performative:** It's often used to justify time spent rather than results achieved.
3. **"Busy" is demoralizing:** It implies overwhelm and a lack of control, which can lead to burnout and disengagement.

Instead of asking, **"Are you busy?"** start asking, **"What are you focusing on?"** or **"What progress have we made?"** These shifts in language push teams toward clarity and intentionality, driving them to prioritize productivity over activity.

Leadership's Role in Eradicating "Busy"

As a leader, it's your responsibility to model and foster an environment where productivity thrives. This means:

- **Setting priorities:** Clearly define what matters most and ensure the team is aligned around those goals.
- **Creating focus:** Encourage time-blocking, reduce unnecessary meetings, and eliminate distractions.
- **Rewarding outcomes, not effort:** Celebrate results, not how many hours someone worked or how "busy" they appeared to be.

Here's the truth: if you let "busy" dominate your team's culture, you're robbing them of the opportunity to excel. The antidote to busy isn't working harder—it's working smarter, with intention and clarity.

Let's stop glorifying busyness and start championing productivity. Your team doesn't need to be busy; they need to be focused, impactful, and successful. It starts with you

Prioritizing Techniques When Your Desk is All "Urgent"

We do live in a world where **everything feels urgent.** Emails ping relentlessly, deadlines loom ominously, and your list of "must-dos" grows faster than you can tackle it. But here's the hard truth: **not all tasks are created equal.** The ability to prioritize isn't just a skill—it's a survival tool for leaders. It's the difference between staying afloat in the chaos and drowning in it.

Effective leaders excel at prioritizing, especially when everything seems equally pressing. It's about cutting through the noise to identify what truly matters. And while the Eisenhower Matrix is one of the most well-known tools, there are other effective techniques that can help you stay focused and intentional in your approach.

The Eisenhower Matrix: A Simple, Powerful Framework

One of the most tried-and-true prioritization techniques is the **Eisenhower Matrix.** This simple tool categorizes tasks into four quadrants, helping you distinguish between what's urgent and important versus what's noise:

1. **Urgent and Important:** These tasks demand immediate action—critical deadlines, pressing crises, or high-stakes decisions.
   - **Action:** Do these first and without delay.
2. **Important but Not Urgent:** These tasks contribute to long-term goals, like strategic planning, skill development, or relationship building.
   - **Action:** Schedule time to address these proactively.
3. **Urgent but Not Important:** These are tasks that feel pressing—emails, interruptions, or minor requests—but don't add significant value.
   - **Action:** Delegate these to someone else.
4. **Neither Urgent nor Important:** These are time-wasters—low-value activities or distractions that don't move the needle.
   - **Action:** Eliminate them entirely.

The Eisenhower Matrix isn't revolutionary, but it's transformational. **It provides clarity and control** when everything feels equally urgent.

Beyond the Matrix: Exploring Other Prioritization Techniques

While the Eisenhower Matrix is a great starting point, it's not a one-size-fits-all solution. Here are additional techniques that can help you manage competing priorities effectively:

1. The ABC Method

Rank tasks as A, B, or C based on their level of importance:

- **A tasks:** Critical and directly tied to goals—must be done immediately.
- **B tasks:** Important but not time-sensitive—schedule them.
- **C tasks:** Nice-to-haves or low-priority items—defer or delegate.

This technique ensures you spend your time on what matters most, rather than what feels most urgent.

2. Pareto Principle (80/20 Rule)

Focus on the **20% of tasks that deliver 80% of the results.** This rule encourages leaders to identify the high-leverage activities that drive the most impact and deprioritize low-value tasks.

3. MIT (Most Important Task)

Begin each day by identifying your **single most important task**—the one thing that will make the biggest difference. Tackle it first before distractions and minor tasks consume your energy.

4. Time-Value Analysis

Evaluate tasks based on the value they bring relative to the time they require. Prioritize high-value tasks that align with strategic objectives, and avoid tasks that consume time but offer little return.

Daily Planning: A Non-Negotiable Leadership Habit

Prioritization doesn't happen by accident—it's an intentional practice. Start each day with a **planning session** that identifies your top priorities. Ask yourself:

- What tasks align with our strategic goals?
- Which activities have the highest impact on the team or organization?
- What can I delegate or defer without compromising results?

Daily planning isn't about adding tasks to your to-do list—it's about subtracting the noise. Focus on **high-impact activities** that create value. According to McKinsey & Company, **41% of time spent by leaders is misallocated to low-priority tasks.** By reclaiming that time, you shift from being busy to being effective.

The Ability to Prioritize: The Leader's Differentiator

Let's be clear: **prioritization separates leaders who fall subject to busy from those who own productivity.** Busy leaders get trapped in the weeds, tackling low-value tasks and putting out fires. Effective leaders step back, evaluate what matters, and focus their energy on driving impact.

Here's the truth: leadership is as much about **what you choose not to do** as it is about what you do. Whether you're using the Eisenhower Matrix, the 80/20 Rule, or simply focusing on your most important task, prioritization forces you to focus on what truly drives success.

Practical Processes to Reclaim Focus

1. **Start with Strategic Alignment:** Every task should tie back to a broader organizational goal. If it doesn't, ask why it's on your list in the first place.

2. **Batch Similar Tasks:** Group similar activities (like emails or administrative work) together to minimize context-switching and maximize efficiency.

3. **Review Your Priorities Weekly:** Take time to evaluate your workload at the end of each week. Adjust as needed to ensure alignment with long-term objectives.

Prioritization isn't about checking boxes—it's about **making better decisions** with your time and energy. It ensures that the hours you invest translate into meaningful results. Tools like the Eisenhower Matrix and techniques like the 80/20 Rule help you cut through the chaos and focus on what truly drives success.

The bottom line? **Leaders don't have the luxury of being busy for the sake of feeling like things are getting done.** Your job is to drive impact. And that starts with mastering the art of prioritization.

Time Management The Great Equalizer

How often in a day do you hear. "Do you have time?" Let's talk about the one resource every leader has in equal measure: **time.** It doesn't matter how brilliant your ideas are, how large your team is, or how much experience you bring to the table—**you get the same 24 hours as everyone else.** What separates great leaders from mediocre ones is how they manage those hours.

Time management isn't about doing everything; it's about **doing the right things at the right time.** It's about focusing your energy where it matters most and creating systems that protect your attention and productivity. Leadership demands intentionality, and nowhere is that more critical than in how you manage your time.

The Myth of Multitasking

Before diving into more processes, let's debunk a myth that's long overdue for the trash heap: **multitasking.** If you think juggling five tasks at once makes you a productivity ninja, think again.

Research from the American Psychological Association reveals that **task-switching can reduce productivity by up to 40%.** Why? Because every time you switch tasks, your brain needs to refocus, burning time and energy in the process. The result isn't better output—it's fragmented thinking and sloppy results.

Lesson: Stop trying to multitask. Instead, focus on one task at a time, execute it with excellence, and then move on to the next.

The Power of Time-Blocking

One of the most effective time management processes for leaders is **time-blocking.** This practice involves dedicating specific, uninterrupted blocks of time to your highest-priority work. Time-blocking is more than a scheduling tool—it's a way to protect your focus and ensure your day aligns with your goals.

What Are Time Blocks?

Time blocks are pre-scheduled periods where you commit to working on specific tasks or categories of work without distraction. Instead of bouncing between tasks, checking emails, or getting pulled into low-priority activities, you focus on one critical task during a defined window of time.

Time-blocking isn't just about planning—it's about execution. When done right, it creates a structure where you can make intentional progress on high-impact activities while also managing recurring tasks effectively.

Why Time-Blocking Works

Eliminates Decision Fatigue: When your priorities are already scheduled, you avoid the mental drain of deciding what to focus on next.

Protects Focus: By batching tasks and setting boundaries, you minimize interruptions and multitasking, both of which are productivity killers.

Prevents Overcommitment: Time-blocking forces you to realistically assess how much you can accomplish in a day, preventing the common trap of overloading your schedule.

Builds Discipline: Consistently using time blocks helps reinforce habits of focus and intentional work.

How to Time-Block Like a Pro

1. Schedule Strategy and Vision Work:
Block time for high-level thinking, planning, and long-term strategic work. This is essential leadership time where you assess direction, review goals, and ensure you're steering your team effectively. If you're always reacting, you're not leading.

Pro Tip: Schedule this block during your peak energy hours when your mind is sharpest. For most people, this is early in the morning.

2. Team Check-Ins and One-on-Ones:
Time-block regular, consistent meetings for team check-ins and one-on-ones. These conversations are essential for maintaining alignment, giving feedback, and building trust within your team. Skipping these blocks can lead to communication breakdowns and misaligned expectations.

Pro Tip: Reserve time for pre-meeting preparation to ensure your check-ins are productive and focused.

3. Creative Problem-Solving and Deep Work:
Dedicate uninterrupted blocks for creative, strategic tasks that require full focus—like brainstorming, writing, or complex decision-making. These tasks demand deeper thinking and can't be accomplished effectively when you're multitasking.

Pro Tip: Silence notifications, close your email, and block external distractions during these sessions. Treat this block as non-negotiable, just like an important meeting.

4. Administrative and Routine Tasks:
Block time for lower-priority tasks like emails, reporting, and administrative duties. These tasks are necessary but shouldn't consume prime productivity hours.

Pro Tip: Batch similar tasks together. For example, schedule a 30-minute window each afternoon for email management instead of checking it constantly throughout the day.

5. Buffer Blocks for Flexibility:
Unexpected issues will arise. Build buffer blocks into your calendar to manage reactive tasks, last-minute meetings, or overflow from previous blocks. This flexibility prevents your schedule from falling apart when disruptions occur.

Pro Tip: Protect buffer blocks—don't let them become a dumping ground for low-priority tasks.

Common Time-Blocking Mistakes (and How to Avoid Them)

Overfilling Your Schedule: Leave space for breaks and unexpected tasks. An overpacked schedule leads to burnout.

Lack of Specificity: Don't just block "Work Time"—label the block with the task you're focusing on to create clarity and accountability.

Ignoring Energy Levels: Align tasks with your energy flow throughout the day. Tackle deep work during peak energy times and lighter tasks when energy dips.

Failing to Protect Time Blocks: Treat your time blocks as sacred appointments. If you constantly let others disrupt them, the system loses its power.

Why It Matters for Leaders

Time-blocking is more than just a productivity hack—it's a leadership discipline. It allows you to prioritize the work that truly matters: setting direction, developing your team, and focusing on strategic growth. Without intentional time management, it's easy to get caught in the day-to-day noise instead of leading with clarity and focus.

The bottom line? You don't need more time—you need better control of your time. Time-blocking helps you lead by design, not by default.

Learning How to Say "No" in a Professional Manner

Let's start with the truth: **we don't say "no" enough.** The number one reason? We haven't given ourselves—or our teams—a compelling reason to say it. Saying no isn't just about declining a task or rejecting an idea; it's about protecting focus, ensuring alignment, and maintaining energy for what matters most. **Saying "yes" to something, means saying "no" to something else.**

If you and your team are struggling to say no, it's time to revisit **Clarity of Purpose** (see Chapter 1). A clear and compelling vision creates a framework for decision-making. When your goals are tied directly to that vision—measurable, time-bound, and prioritized—you don't need to justify your no. It becomes self-evident.

Leaders who can say no effectively help their teams do the same. **Your role as a leader isn't just to manage tasks—it's to ensure everyone's energy is directed toward impactful work.** Saying no is not about rejection; it's about focus.

Why Leaders Must Say "No"

Saying yes to everything might feel like you're being supportive, approachable, or collaborative. But here's the reality: **saying yes to everything is a fast track to burnout and mediocrity.** It dilutes your energy, spreads your team too thin, and reduces the quality of your output.

Leaders who say yes to everything create chaos, not clarity. Worse, they send the message that every request is equally important, leaving teams overwhelmed and directionless. **Saying no strategically is an essential leadership skill—one that protects your team's ability to execute consistently and at a high level.**

Why no matters:

1. **It Maintains Focus:** Saying no keeps your team aligned with priorities that drive the most significant results.
2. **It Reduces Burnout:** Protecting bandwidth ensures your team has the capacity to deliver their best work without running themselves into the ground.

3. **It Builds Credibility:** Leaders who say no strategically gain trust and respect for their ability to protect the team and stay focused on high-value work.

How to Say "No" with Clarity and Respect

Saying no effectively requires tact, professionalism, and empathy. It's not just about turning someone down—it's about doing so in a way that maintains relationships and reinforces priorities.

Here's how to say no the right way:

1. **Be Clear and Respectful**
   - Ambiguity weakens your message. Be direct but respectful, explaining why the task or request doesn't align with current goals.
   - Example: "This initiative is valuable, but it doesn't align with our strategic objectives for the quarter. We need to stay focused on delivering the product launch on time."
2. **Tie Back to the Vision**
   - Reinforce your decision by connecting it to the bigger picture. This shows that the no isn't personal—it's strategic.
   - Example: "To achieve our annual growth target, we need to prioritize resources on initiatives that directly impact our customer acquisition goals. This request, while important, doesn't align with that focus right now."
3. **Offer Alternatives**
   - When possible, provide constructive solutions. Suggest a revised timeline, a different resource, or someone else who might be better equipped to handle the task.
   - Example: "I can't take this on right now, but let's revisit it next quarter when we'll have more capacity. In the meantime, I suggest discussing it with [specific team member], who may be able to support it sooner."

4. **Empathize Without Overcommitting**
    - Acknowledge the importance of the request and show you understand its value, but remain firm in your decision.
    - Example: "I know this is a priority for you, and I appreciate the effort you've put into it. Right now, our focus needs to remain on [specific initiative]. Let's brainstorm ways to address this in the future."

Building a Culture of Strategic "No"

Saying no isn't just a skill for leaders—it's a **cultural value** that protects your team's energy, time, and focus. When you model strategic decision-making, you give your team permission to say no to distractions and stay committed to what matters most.

Here's how to foster a culture of strategic no:

1. **Empower Decision-Making:** Encourage your team to assess whether tasks align with their goals. Give them the confidence to decline requests that don't add value.
2. **Celebrate Smart Decisions:** Recognize and reward team members who prioritize effectively and protect their bandwidth.
3. **Define Non-Negotiables:** Make sure your team knows what's most important. Clear priorities make it easier for them to determine when a no is appropriate.

Saying yes might feel good in the moment, but over time, it erodes focus, spreads your team too thin, and sacrifices quality. Leaders who say no effectively—and teach their teams to do the same—create space for meaningful, impactful work.

Saying no isn't about rejection; it's about **protection.** It protects your team's energy, ensures alignment with your vision, and reinforces a culture where effort is directed toward high-value tasks.

The bottom line? A leader who knows how to say no strategically is a leader who drives results without burning out their team. **Every no creates space for a more impactful yes.**

Why Failing to Delegate is a Big, Big Mistake

Here's the blunt truth: **if you're not delegating, you're being selfish.** What? By keeping everything on your plate, you're not just overburdening yourself—you're **stealing from your team.** You're stealing their opportunities for growth, their chance to develop new skills, and even their right to learn through failure. Leadership isn't about hoarding responsibilities; it's about creating space for others to step up, contribute, and thrive.

Failing to delegate doesn't make you a hero—it makes you a bottleneck. It sends the message that you don't trust your team or believe in their abilities. Worse, it deprives them of the chance to take ownership, build confidence, and learn from their experiences. As a leader, your job is to guide and empower—not to do it all yourself.

Delegation: The Multiplier Effect

Delegation isn't just about offloading tasks you don't want to do; it's about **scaling your leadership.** It's how you free yourself to focus on strategic priorities while simultaneously investing in your team's growth. Done right, delegation creates a ripple effect: it multiplies your impact, strengthens your team, and builds a culture of trust and accountability.

Here's why delegation matters:

1. **It Builds Capacity:** The more you delegate, the more your team can accomplish collectively, allowing the organization to achieve bigger goals.

2. **It Develops Talent:** Delegation gives your team members the chance to stretch beyond their comfort zones, build new skills, and gain confidence.

3. **It Fosters Trust:** Delegation says, **"I believe in you."** It creates a foundation of trust and signals to your team that you see their potential.

How to Delegate Effectively

Delegation isn't just about handing off work—it's about doing so intentionally and strategically. Here's how to delegate in a way that empowers your team and ensures success:

1. **Match Tasks with Skills**
   - Take the time to assess your team's strengths, interests, and areas for growth. Assign tasks that align with their capabilities and stretch them appropriately.
   - Example: A team member with strong analytical skills? Assign them a data-driven project. Someone passionate about communication? Let them lead a client presentation.

2. **Provide Clear Instructions and Expectations**
   - Ambiguity kills delegation. Be explicit about what needs to be done, why it matters, and what success looks like.
   - Example: "Your goal is to create a client-facing report that highlights our Q3 results. Focus on three key metrics: revenue growth, customer retention, and cost savings. Let's review a draft by next Wednesday."

3. **Empower Ownership**
   - Delegation isn't about micromanaging—it's about handing over responsibility. Give your team members the autonomy to make decisions within their scope and own the outcome.
   - Example: "This is your project to lead. I trust your judgment—bring me any roadblocks, but otherwise, it's yours to run with."

4. **Check In Strategically**
   - Follow-up isn't about hovering; it's about supporting. Schedule regular touchpoints to offer guidance, address obstacles, and ensure progress.
   - Example: "Let's touch base every Monday for a quick check-in to see how things are progressing and tackle any challenges together."

The Cost of Not Delegating

By refusing to delegate, leaders create a bottleneck that stifles progress —not just for the team, but for themselves. The cost is significant:

- **Overwhelm:** Leaders who try to do it all burn out and lose sight of their strategic priorities.
- **Underdevelopment:** Team members miss out on opportunities to learn, grow, and take ownership of their work.
- **Distrust:** A lack of delegation signals to your team that you don't trust them, undermining morale and engagement.

Delegation and Trust

Delegation isn't just a tool—it's a **trust exercise.** When you delegate effectively, you're not just distributing work; you're building relationships and fostering a culture of accountability. According to Gallup, **employees who feel trusted and empowered are 23% more likely to exceed expectations.**

Leaders who fail to delegate aren't just limiting themselves—they're limiting their teams. By keeping tasks you should hand off, you're robbing others of the chance to grow, take risks, and learn through both success and failure.

Delegation isn't just about getting more done—it's about **investing in your people.** It's how you create a high-performing team that thrives, learns, and takes ownership of its success. And it's how you free yourself to focus on what matters most: leading with clarity, purpose, and impact.

The bottom line? Delegation isn't just a leadership skill—it's a leadership responsibility. **Stop stealing opportunities from your team and start empowering them to succeed.**

Building Momentum

Consistency isn't just about effort—it's about **creating momentum.** Momentum is the invisible force that turns small wins into major victories, transforming one productive day into a streak of success. It's not something that happens by chance; it's something leaders build intentionally.

Momentum doesn't just drive results; it creates energy and enthusiasm within a team. It's what separates leaders who are effective in the short term from those who build sustainable, high-performing cultures. Momentum creates a rhythm of productivity and progress that becomes self-sustaining, lifting individuals and teams to new heights.

How to Build Momentum

Momentum isn't magic—it's the product of intentional actions that inspire trust, focus, and progress. Here's how to build it:

1. Celebrate Small Wins

Recognizing progress isn't just a "feel-good" tactic—it's a proven way to keep morale high and motivation strong. Celebrating small wins reinforces positive behavior and shows your team that their efforts are valued.

Action Step: Regularly acknowledge milestones, even if they seem minor. A quick shoutout in a team meeting or a simple email of appreciation can go a long way in maintaining enthusiasm.

Why It Works: According to research from Harvard Business Review, teams that recognize progress daily are more motivated and productive.

2. Set Achievable Milestones

Large goals can feel overwhelming, but breaking them into smaller, manageable steps keeps the team focused and confident. Each milestone achieved becomes fuel for the next, creating a steady rhythm of accomplishment.

Action Step: When tackling a big project, create a timeline with clear, incremental goals. Ensure each milestone is realistic and directly tied to the larger objective.

Why It Works: Studies show that achieving small, measurable goals boosts dopamine levels, reinforcing motivation and engagement.

3. Lead by Example

Momentum starts with the leader. If you show up consistently, execute with discipline, and follow through on your commitments, your team will mirror that behavior. Consistency is contagious, and it begins at the top.

Action Step: Demonstrate the behaviors you want your team to emulate. Be on time, meet deadlines, and deliver results with excellence.

Why It Works: Research from Gallup indicates that teams with consistent leadership are more likely to trust their leaders and maintain high levels of engagement.

4. Maintain Focus During Setbacks

Momentum can be fragile. When setbacks occur, it's crucial to keep your team focused and moving forward. Address issues head-on, but don't let them derail progress.

Action Step: When challenges arise, reframe them as opportunities to learn and adapt. Communicate clearly with your team about the path forward.

Why It Works: Teams that can maintain progress despite setbacks are more resilient and better equipped to handle future challenges.

Momentum is Contagious

Momentum isn't just an individual effort—it's a collective phenomenon. When your team sees progress, they're energized to contribute even more. This creates a virtuous cycle where success breeds success.

Research from the **Journal of Organizational Behavior** found that teams experiencing consistent progress are:

- **31% more engaged.**
- **23% more likely to exceed performance goals.**

Momentum isn't just about results; it's about creating an environment where people feel motivated, empowered, and excited to push forward.

Without consistent execution, even the best strategies fail. Leadership isn't about big, flashy moments—it's about the **quiet discipline of delivering results day after day.** Momentum is what turns that discipline into a force multiplier, driving progress and building trust across your team.

A culture of consistent execution builds trust, credibility, and motivation. It shows your team that leadership isn't just about what you say—it's about what you do. This quadrant of the **Leading by Design** model is the glue that holds everything else together. It's not glamorous, but it's essential.

At the end of the day, leaders are measured not by their intentions but by their outcomes. Or, as every successful leader would say: **just get it done**.

Chapter 3: Takeaways

1. Prioritization is Your Survival Tool

Not all tasks are created equal, and trying to tackle everything is a recipe for chaos. Tools like the **Eisenhower Matrix** and the **80/20 Rule** help leaders cut through the noise, identify high-impact priorities, and focus their energy where it matters most. Great leaders don't just get things done—they get the right things done.

2. Master Time Management

Time is the great equalizer—every leader gets the same 24 hours. The difference lies in how you use them. Techniques like **time-blocking** and leveraging your **peak energy hours** ensure that your most important work gets done when you're at your best. Effective time management isn't about doing more; it's about protecting your focus and maximizing impact.

3. Delegate Like a Leader, Not a Manager

Delegation is about more than offloading tasks—it's about scaling your leadership and empowering your team. When you delegate effectively, you build trust, develop talent, and free yourself to focus on strategic priorities. Remember: if you're not delegating, you're stealing growth opportunities from your team.

4. The Superpower of Saying "No"

Leaders who say yes to everything dilute their focus and spread their teams too thin. Learning to say **no strategically** protects your energy, reinforces priorities, and sets the tone for a culture of focus and high performance. Every no creates space for a more impactful yes.

5. Build and Sustain Momentum

Consistency isn't just effort—it's about creating momentum. Momentum turns small wins into streaks of success and motivates your team to keep pushing forward. Celebrate progress, set achievable milestones, and lead by example to ensure momentum builds and sustains. Momentum is contagious, and it drives engagement and results.

Processes for Implementation

- Prioritization Workshops: Hold workshops on prioritization techniques to help team members learn how to effectively manage their workloads.
- Regular Delegation Reviews: Conduct monthly reviews of delegation practices to ensure tasks are appropriately assigned and supported.
- Time Management Training: Offer training sessions on time management and the benefits of time blocking for enhancing focus and productivity.
- Role-Playing Scenarios for Saying "No": Practice scenarios where leaders and team members can learn to say "no" effectively, helping them handle such situations confidently in real work environments.

By focusing on consistent execution through effective prioritization, time management, delegation, and the ability to professionally refuse non-priority tasks, leaders can ensure that their teams are not only productive but also balanced and less prone to burnout.

Chapter 4
CONNECTION

"People don't care how much you know until they know how much you care."
– Theodore Roosevelt

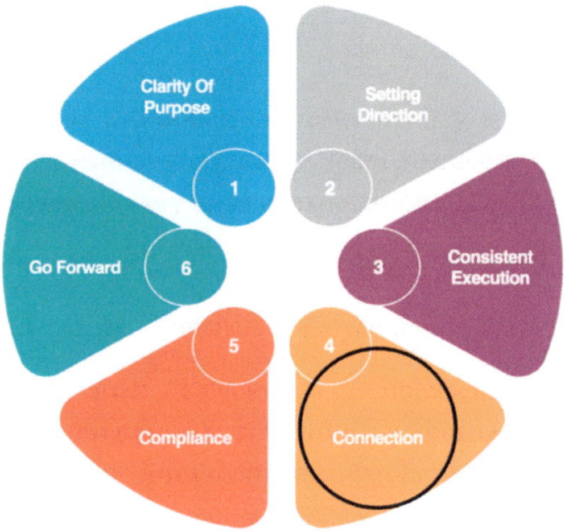

Leadership isn't just about strategy or execution—it's also about people. And yet, every so often, I get pushback: **"You care too much about process. You put too much emphasis on systems and not enough on people."** You know what? Guilty as charged. I do emphasize process.

Why? Because process creates space. It builds a foundation of predictability and efficiency, allowing leaders to focus their most valuable resource—time—on what truly matters: their people.

No matter what industry you're in—whether it's finance, manufacturing, healthcare, or tech—at its core, every business can be distilled down to a series of processes. The way a product gets made, how customers are served, how decisions are made, how teams operate—all of it is process-driven at its foundation. Yet, not all businesses thrive. The ones that rise above the rest aren't just those with innovative products or deep pockets—they're the ones relentlessly committed to mastering and refining their processes.

But here's the key: **it's not just about having processes—it's about being radical about them.** The businesses that win don't leave processes to chance or legacy thinking. They break them down, rebuild them, stress-test them, and continuously improve them. They understand that well-designed, repeatable processes create predictability, efficiency, and scale—allowing them to deliver consistent results in a way their competitors can't match.

However, processes alone don't create success. **The real game-changer? Pairing exceptional processes with extraordinary talent.** Processes set the structure, but it's the people within those processes who drive innovation, performance, and growth. The highest-performing businesses don't just map out how work gets done—they obsess over matching those processes with the right people, putting talent in the right roles where they can have the greatest impact.

This is why **Connection** is the next critical component in the Leading by Design operating model. It's not enough to just have a system or a set of rules in place. Success comes from connecting those processes to the human side of leadership—fostering trust, collaboration, and alignment between the people executing the work and the processes guiding their efforts.

Connection ensures that people feel seen, heard, and valued within the framework of process. It transforms rigid procedures into a thriving ecosystem where feedback, growth, and collaboration can flourish. Because let's face it: even the most brilliant process fails if the people executing it feel disconnected from the purpose behind it.

The businesses that thrive are the ones where process and people work in harmony. When leaders commit to both, they create cultures where process drives results and connection drives engagement—leading to unstoppable performance. That's why Connection isn't just a quadrant in Leading by Design—it's the glue that binds exceptional process with exceptional people, ensuring long-term success and impact.

We live in a demanding, high-performance world. The stakes are high, the pace is relentless, and there's zero margin for error. A solid process isn't just a nice-to-have; it's the safety net that ensures leaders aren't buried in chaos. It delivers a higher level of predictable outcomes, which in turn frees leaders from constantly firefighting. And that's the secret: when you're not bogged down by uncertainty, you can invest your energy where it counts—on the real variables that drive performance: your team.

Here's the thing: **process and people aren't opposites; they're partners.** A well-defined process doesn't diminish the human side of leadership; it amplifies it. It takes care of the noise—the scheduling, the tracking, the mechanics—so leaders can step into the role that no process can replace: inspiring, coaching, and empowering their people.

So, yes, I care deeply about process. Not because it's the endgame, but because it's the enabler. It's the structure that allows leaders to focus less on logistics and more on unlocking the potential of their teams. Process isn't a substitute for connection; it's what makes connection possible.

At its core, leadership is a profoundly human endeavor, and **Connection** is the bridge that links vision to reality, strategy to execution, and individuals to a common purpose. So much so that I created a specific training that only helps team only focus on Connection (Paratus Consulting's CONNECT for Teams). Without connection, leadership becomes hollow—a series of directives and transactions that fail to inspire or engage. With connection, however, leadership transforms into a shared journey, one where people don't just follow because they have to—they commit because they want to.

Connection is what separates great leaders from good managers. Great leaders don't just manage processes; they **inspire people.** They build teams that are cohesive, collaborative, and motivated to achieve not just organizational goals but personal fulfillment. Connection is what turns a group of individuals into a thriving community, bound by trust and loyalty.

Why Connection Matters

Here's the deal: **people don't leave jobs; they leave bad leaders.** A leader who lacks connection might achieve short-term success, but it's a ticking time bomb. Over time, they'll find themselves surrounded by disengaged employees, a culture of apathy, and—eventually—empty desks.

Connection isn't a soft skill—it's process as well. It drives engagement, fosters collaboration, and builds resilience in the face of challenges. A leader who prioritizes connection creates a culture where people bring their best selves to work.

Let's settle a major misconception that plagues the workplace today: **connection is NOT engagement.** These two terms are often thrown around interchangeably, but they couldn't be more different. Conflating the two is one of the reasons so many workplace initiatives fall flat, leaving leaders scratching their heads and wondering why their efforts aren't moving the needle.

Here's the difference: **engagement is an outcome; connection drives that outcome.**

Engagement is about metrics and surveys. It's about how employees feel about their jobs, their managers, or the organization on a surface level. It's often measured by how likely they are to recommend the company or how satisfied they are with their role. And while engagement is important, it's limited. An engaged employee might enjoy their work, but that doesn't mean they feel a deep sense of belonging or commitment to their team or the organization's vision.

Connection, on the other hand, is a deeper, more personal social bond that drives engagement. It's about trust, respect, and alignment with purpose. Connection happens when employees feel truly seen, valued, and understood—not just as workers but as people. When there's connection, employees don't just show up for a paycheck—they show up because they care, because they believe in what they're doing, and because they feel an authentic bond with their team and their leader.

And here's the kicker: connection fuels **psychological safety,** that magic ingredient that allows teams to take risks, innovate, and recover from setbacks without fear of judgment or retribution. Without it, creativity dies, collaboration falters, and performance flatlines.

- **Engagement:** Connected leaders inspire employees to invest emotionally in their work, increasing motivation and satisfaction.
- **Collaboration:** A culture of connection fosters open communication and teamwork, breaking down silos and enabling collective success.
- **Resilience:** Teams that feel connected are more adaptable and supportive, bouncing back faster from challenges.

Building Trust and Loyalty

Trust isn't automatic—it's earned. "**Trust is earned in drops but lost in buckets.**" It's built through **consistency, transparency, and integrity.** Trustworthy leaders say what they mean, do what they say, and own their mistakes. They communicate openly, avoid politics, and never hide behind corporate jargon.

But trust is a two-way street. When leaders demonstrate trust in their teams—by delegating, empowering, and giving them space to succeed—they often find that trust reciprocated in spades. This reciprocal trust builds loyalty, the kind of bond that keeps people committed to the vision even when the going gets tough.

How to Build Trust and Loyalty:

1. **Show Up Consistently:** Be predictable in your actions and words. If you make promises, keep them. If you can't, communicate why.
2. **Communicate Authentically:** People can smell insincerity a mile away. Speak with honesty and humility—your team will respect you for it.
3. **Empower Your Team:** Trust your team with meaningful responsibilities. Delegation isn't just about sharing the workload; it's about showing your confidence in their abilities.
4. **Own Your Mistakes:** No one expects perfection. When you make a mistake, acknowledge it, learn from it, and move forward. Accountability earns respect.

Pro Tip: Don't just assume trust exists. **Invest in it.** Spend time in one-on-one conversations. Ask for feedback—and mean it. Show your team that you're not just their boss—you're their advocate.

Connection is the Catalyst for Transformation

Connection isn't just about making people feel good—it's about creating an environment where they can thrive. Connected teams don't just comply; they commit. They don't just perform; they innovate. And they don't just show up; they bring their whole selves to the table.

Leadership without connection is like a bridge without supports—it might hold up for a while, but it's destined to collapse. With connection, leadership becomes transformational, turning everyday work into a shared vision.

Connection Intelligence

You were introduced at the beginning of this book to the **three pillars** of how leaders execute the process of leadership: teaching, challenging, and role modeling. These pillars are embedded within every aspect of leadership, including the **Leading by Design** model.

Leadership, at its core, is an emotional business. It's not just about hitting KPIs or driving results—it's about navigating the messy, complex, and deeply human aspects of working with people. While **emotional intelligence (EQ)** has been a buzzword for years, its reputation as "soft and squishy" often leaves leaders confused about how to apply it in practical, actionable ways.

That's where **Connection Intelligence** comes in. It's not just a concept; it's a framework for leaders to build genuine trust, inspire their teams, and create a culture that thrives. Connection intelligence is the way we use **Teach. Challenge. and or Role Model** to execute our leadership. Connection Intelligence brings clarity and structure to the emotional side of leadership, making it accessible and actionable for anyone ready to lead by design.

Connection Intelligence isn't just a rebrand of EQ; it's a framework for turning emotional awareness into actionable leadership. It's about bridging the gap between empathy and execution, creating a culture where people feel understood, valued, and empowered to contribute their best. Within the leading by design framework the connective tissue that binds it all together is a leaders ability to have connection intelligence and bring teams together.

What is Connection Intelligence?

At its core, Connection Intelligence is the ability to **engage deeply with your team while driving them toward a shared purpose.** *How do we Teach? How do we Challenge? How do we Role Model?* It's not just about understanding emotions, but then how we deliver—it's about using that understanding to build trust, foster collaboration, and inspire action. At this point is where most people ask me well, how do

I connect as a leader?, how do I build that trust? It's a skill you can develop, and the best way to build it is through the **Three-Pillar Model within Leading by Design: Teach, Challenge, and Role Model.**

The Three Pillars of Connection Intelligence

1. Teach Them

Leadership isn't just about directing traffic; it's about imparting knowledge, perspective, and purpose. Teaching is how you connect your team to the "why" behind the work. It's how you equip them with the tools and understanding they need to thrive.

Great leaders teach their teams not just *what* to do but *why* it matters. When people understand the bigger picture, their work stops being transactional and starts being meaningful.

Processes to Employ:

- **Host Regular Learning Opportunities:** Schedule training sessions, workshops, or lunch-and-learns to share skills and knowledge.
- **Share Insights During Meetings:** Use team check-ins to provide relevant information, industry trends, or lessons learned.
- **Give Constructive Feedback:** Feedback isn't just a performance tool; it's a teaching moment. Focus on growth, not just correction.
- **Foster Peer Learning:** Encourage team members to share their expertise and learn from each other.

Example: Instead of just assigning a project, explain how it aligns with the company's strategic goals. Help your team see how their contribution fits into the bigger picture.

2. Challenge Them

The best leaders don't just hand out tasks—they **push their teams to grow.** Challenges inspire innovation, build confidence, and reveal untapped potential. When leaders challenge their teams, they're not just assigning work—they're creating opportunities for development.

Challenging your team isn't about setting impossible expectations; it's about presenting meaningful tasks that require them to stretch their skills and mindset.

Processes to Employ:

- **Assign Stretch Projects:** Give team members responsibilities slightly outside their comfort zones to help them grow.
- **Encourage Creative Problem-Solving:** Ask open-ended questions that force your team to think beyond the obvious.
- **Provide Support, Not Answers:** Offer resources and guidance but let your team navigate challenges independently.
- **Celebrate Effort, Not Just Success:** Recognize the courage it takes to tackle tough tasks, even if the outcomes aren't perfect.

Example: When a team member says they aren't ready for a leadership opportunity, challenge them to take the role with your support. Help them see failure as a stepping stone, not a dead end.

3. Be a Role Model

If teaching is the "why" and challenging is the "how," **role modeling is the "show."** Leadership isn't just about telling your team what to do—it's about showing them how to do it. Your behavior sets the tone for your team's culture, work ethic, and values.

The best leaders understand that actions speak louder than words. If you want your team to show integrity, resilience, or creativity, you need to live those traits yourself.

Processes to Employ:

- **Lead with Integrity:** Be honest, transparent, and consistent in your decisions and actions.

- **Show Commitment:** Demonstrate your dedication to the team's goals through your effort and focus.
- **Handle Setbacks Gracefully:** When things go wrong, model resilience and adaptability. Your response will set the tone for the team.
- **Practice Empathy:** Show that you value your team members as people, not just workers. Listen, understand, and respect their perspectives.

Example: If you expect your team to prioritize self-improvement, show them you're doing the same by sharing your learning journey or seeking their feedback.

Connection Intelligence turns emotional awareness into leadership impact. It's not just about identifying feelings or understanding team dynamics—it's about taking action that builds trust, inspires commitment, and creates meaningful relationships. Le verging the three pillars of Teaching, Challenging. And Role Modeling to drive for deeper connection.

Without connection, leadership becomes transactional—a give-and-take relationship that might hit short-term goals but fails to inspire long-term loyalty or engagement. With connection, leadership becomes transformational—a shared journey toward a common vision where people feel empowered to bring their best.

Discussion: Putting Connection Intelligence into Action

Here's the question: **How can you use one of these pillars—Teach, Challenge, or Role Model—right now with your team or a group you're trying to lead?**

Start small. Whether it's explaining the "why" behind a project, assigning a stretch goal, or demonstrating resilience in the face of a challenge, your actions will set the tone for connection.

Connection Intelligence isn't a theory—it's a practice. When you teach, challenge, and role model every day, you're not just building connection—you're building a team that's committed, inspired, and ready to thrive.

Transforming Teams into Communities

Over time the objective of connection is to great a community. I love the thought: **A true measure of connection? If they still wear your T-shirt after they leave.** A connected team isn't just a group of people working together—it's a **community.** Communities aren't defined by job titles or shared office spaces; they're built on trust, shared values, and a sense of belonging. When teams evolve into communities, the dynamic shifts: coworkers become allies, challenges become opportunities, and the workplace becomes a space where people want to be, not just where they have to be.

At the heart of building a community is **establishing rituals and traditions** that create shared experiences and reinforce the team's identity. Communities thrive on consistency, celebration, and connection—things that can be intentionally fostered through regular practices and touchpoints.

Why Community Matters

Without connection you won't have community, a team is just a group of individuals completing tasks. Functional, yes, but uninspired. On the other hand, when a team feels like a community, the energy changes:

- **Stronger Bonds:** Team members look out for one another, creating an environment of trust and mutual support.
- **Increased Engagement:** Communities inspire emotional investment, leading to greater motivation and enthusiasm.
- **Resilience:** In tough times, communities rally together, supporting each other through challenges.

- **Shared Purpose:** Communities align around a common vision, making their efforts more cohesive and impactful.

Connection is the glue that holds communities together, but rituals and traditions are what make the glue stick.

Building Rituals and Traditions: The Foundation of Community

Rituals and traditions create rhythm and meaning within a team. They provide predictable touchpoints that foster camaraderie and help teams celebrate their shared identity. Here's how leaders can intentionally establish rituals and traditions to transform their teams into thriving communities:

1. Start with Weekly Check-Ins

Consistency is key to building connection. A weekly check-in ritual creates space for open communication, reflection, and alignment.

Processes to Try:

- **Wins and Challenges:** Begin each week with a team huddle where everyone shares one win and one challenge. This fosters transparency and encourages mutual support.
- **Themes of the Week:** Kick off the week by aligning the team around a theme or focus, such as "collaboration" or "creative problem-solving."
- **Intentional Listening:** Use these moments to listen actively and address concerns, ensuring everyone feels heard and valued.

2. Celebrate Team Successes Together

Communities thrive on celebration. Recognizing both individual and collective achievements reinforces a sense of belonging and motivates the team to aim higher.

Processes to Try:

- **Milestone Moments:** Celebrate project completions, hitting team goals, or anniversaries with small, meaningful gestures like a catered lunch or virtual toast.
- **Recognition Rituals:** Create a tradition of giving "shoutouts" during meetings or via team channels to spotlight individual contributions.
- **End-of-Week Wins:** Close out each week by reflecting on progress and acknowledging the team's hard work.

3. Build Cultural Touchstones

Cultural touchstones—shared experiences that reflect the team's identity—anchor the team's sense of community. These don't have to be extravagant; they just need to be meaningful.

Processes to Try:

- **First Fridays:** Host a casual gathering on the first Friday of every month, whether it's coffee chats, virtual trivia, or a team lunch.
- **Team Playlists:** Build a shared playlist where everyone contributes their favorite songs, creating a fun and personal soundtrack for the workplace.
- **Personalized Traditions:** Ask team members to share their ideas for new rituals, from book club sessions to themed dress days.

4. Create Shared Learning Opportunities

Communities grow when their members grow. Establish rituals that prioritize learning and development to build a sense of shared progress and purpose.

Processes to Try:

- **Knowledge Swaps:** Dedicate one meeting a month to having team members teach each other something new—whether work-related or personal.

- **Lunch-and-Learns:** Bring in guest speakers or have team members present on topics they're passionate about.
- **Skill-Sharing Sessions:** Rotate responsibility for leading workshops on tools, systems, or strategies that benefit the team.

5. Mark Milestones with Meaning

Milestones deserve more than a passing mention—they're opportunities to bring the team closer together. Ritualizing these moments creates shared memories and reinforces the value of collaboration.

Processes to Try:

- **Project Launches:** Celebrate the start of a new project with a kickoff event that builds excitement and alignment.
- **Goal Achievement Parties:** When the team hits a major milestone, make it a big deal—bring in snacks, write personalized thank-you notes, or even take a team outing.
- **Year-in-Review Traditions:** Dedicate the last meeting of the year to reflecting on accomplishments, sharing gratitude, and setting intentions for the future.

Why These Rituals Matter

Rituals and traditions may seem small, but their impact is massive. They create the emotional glue that transforms individual contributors into a cohesive community. When people feel connected through shared experiences, they're more likely to trust one another, support one another, and go above and beyond for the collective good.

Rituals are the reminders that:

- **We're in this together.**
- **Our work has meaning.**
- **Our contributions matter.**

Connection is the Key to Community

Building a connected team isn't just about processes or performance metrics—it's about creating spaces where people feel they belong. Communities aren't just efficient; they're **engaged, resilient, and committed** to a shared vision. As a leader, your job isn't just to manage tasks; it's to build an environment where your team becomes a community, united by trust, rituals, and purpose.

Transform your team into a community, and you'll create something that lasts.

Addressing Attitudes

What works against connection? Early in my career, I had a mediocre manager—not a leader—who influenced me profoundly in terms of what I didn't want to become as a leader. However, one lesson he instilled in me still holds true today: **hire for attitude first, then skill.** Skills can be trained, but retraining attitude? That's a far more challenging—if not impossible—task.

A single bad attitude can poison a team. Whether it's negativity, disengagement, or outright hostility, attitude problems don't just affect the individual—they ripple through the team, undermining morale, productivity, and trust. Leaders can't afford to ignore these issues, nor can they afford to mishandle them. Addressing attitude problems proactively and effectively is essential for maintaining a healthy, high-performing work environment.

Here's the deal: attitude problems are rarely about the work itself. They often stem from deeper frustrations—feeling undervalued, misunderstood, or disconnected from the team's purpose. As a leader, your job isn't just to spot the symptoms; it's to uncover and address the root causes.

Step 1: Early Identification

The first rule of managing attitude problems? **Catch them early.** Letting negativity fester is like ignoring a leak in your roof—it won't fix itself, and it'll cause a lot more damage if left unchecked.

How to Spot Attitude Problems Early:

1. **Behavioral Shifts:** Look for changes in tone, body language, or work habits. A once-engaged team member who becomes withdrawn or combative is waving a red flag.

2. **Team Feedback:** Pay attention to what others are saying. If team members mention tension or lack of collaboration, dig deeper.

3. **Performance Metrics:** Declining output or missed deadlines can often be a symptom of disengagement or frustration.

Pro Tip: Don't wait for a major blowup. If something feels off, address it sooner rather than later. Small course corrections now can prevent larger issues down the road.

Step 2: Empathetic Engagement

Here's the truth: **you can't fix what you don't understand.** Before jumping to conclusions, take the time to understand the underlying causes of an attitude problem. Approach the situation with empathy, not judgment.

How to Engage with Empathy:

- **Ask, Don't Assume:** Initiate a one-on-one conversation with open-ended questions. "I've noticed you've seemed a bit disengaged lately—what's been on your mind?" shows concern without accusation.

- **Listen Actively:** Don't just wait for your turn to speak. Really hear what the person is saying, both in their words and in their tone.

- **Acknowledge Feelings:** Validate their perspective, even if you don't agree with it. "I can see how that situation would feel frustrating" goes a long way in building trust.
- **Identify Barriers:** Work together to uncover what's standing in the way of their engagement—whether it's workload, conflict with a colleague, or a lack of clarity about expectations.

Step 3: Constructive Feedback

Once you understand the root cause, it's time to address the behavior —but how you frame your feedback matters. Feedback that feels like a personal attack will only escalate the issue. **The goal is to be specific, constructive, and solutions-oriented.**

How to Provide Effective Feedback:

1. **Focus on Behaviors, Not Personal Traits:** Instead of saying, "You're being difficult," say, "I noticed you interrupted several teammates during the meeting. Let's talk about how we can create a more collaborative discussion."
2. **Be Specific:** Vague feedback doesn't help. Pinpoint the behaviors that need to change and explain why they're problematic.
3. **Tie it to Impact:** Help them see how their actions affect the team. "When deadlines are missed, it creates stress for everyone. Let's discuss how we can better align expectations moving forward."
4. **Collaborate on Solutions:** Feedback isn't a one-way street. Invite them to share their perspective and brainstorm ways to move forward together.

Pro Tip: Frame feedback as an opportunity for growth. When people feel supported, they're more likely to respond positively to constructive criticism.

Step 4: Create a Path Forward

Addressing an attitude problem isn't a one-and-done conversation. It's about creating a plan for improvement and holding the individual accountable while providing the support they need to succeed.

How to Build a Plan for Improvement:

- **Set Clear Expectations:** Define what "better" looks like. Be explicit about the behaviors you expect moving forward.
- **Schedule Check-Ins:** Regularly touch base to discuss progress, provide additional feedback, and adjust the plan as needed.
- **Offer Resources:** If the issue stems from skill gaps, burnout, or personal challenges, provide access to training, coaching, or time off.
- **Recognize Progress:** Acknowledge improvements, no matter how small. Positive reinforcement can cement the changes you're looking for.

Attitude problems aren't just about the individual—they're about the team. Left unchecked, negativity spreads like a virus, draining morale and creating a toxic environment. But when leaders address these issues with empathy, clarity, and consistency, they can turn potential liabilities into opportunities for growth.

Bottom Line: Combating attitude problems isn't just about resolving conflict—it's about building trust, improving team dynamics, and reinforcing the culture of connection that every great team needs to thrive.

Addressing Conflict with Confidence

Another source of connection erosion is unresolved or unhealthy conflict. Let's face it: **conflict is inevitable.** No matter how cohesive or high-performing your team may be, clashes will occur. Personalities will collide, strategies will diverge, and expectations will occasionally fall short. The question isn't whether conflict will happen—it's how you, as a leader, will handle it when it does.

Here's the thing: **conflict isn't inherently bad.** Handled well, it can spark innovation, strengthen relationships, and clarify misunderstandings. Handled poorly—or avoided altogether—it can fester into resentment, disengagement, or outright dysfunction. Great leaders don't dodge conflict; they **lean into it** with confidence, empathy, and a focus on resolution.

Why Conflict is an Opportunity

While conflict can feel uncomfortable, it's also a **sign of engagement.** Teams that care deeply about their work will inevitably have disagreements. The key is to channel that passion constructively rather than letting it become destructive.

What great leaders understand:

- **Conflict is a signal, not a problem.** It often points to deeper issues—misaligned expectations, unclear roles, or unmet needs—that need addressing.
- **Conflict can build trust.** When handled openly and respectfully, it shows team members that their voices matter and that differing perspectives are valued.
- **Conflict drives clarity.** Resolving disagreements often leads to sharper strategies, better communication, and stronger alignment.

How to Address Conflict with Confidence

1. Act Early: Don't Let Conflict Fester

Unresolved conflict is like a leaky pipe—it doesn't get better with time, and the damage only worsens. Addressing issues early prevents minor disagreements from escalating into major blowouts.

Action Step: When you notice tension, initiate a conversation. Start with curiosity: "I've sensed some friction around [specific issue]. Can we talk about it?"

2. Lead with Empathy and Curiosity

The goal isn't to prove who's right—it's to understand differing perspectives. Empathy doesn't mean agreeing with everyone; it means respecting where they're coming from.

Action Step: Listen actively. Ask open-ended questions like, "Can you help me understand your perspective on this?" Acknowledge emotions without letting them derail the conversation.

3. Focus on Behaviors, Not Personalities

Personal attacks escalate conflict; focusing on specific behaviors keeps the conversation productive. Shift the narrative from "you always" to "when this happens."

Action Step: Instead of saying, "You're too critical in meetings," say, "When feedback is given in a harsh tone, it's harder for the team to feel comfortable contributing."

4. Seek Solutions, Not Blame

Blame might feel satisfying in the moment, but it rarely resolves anything. Shift the focus to finding common ground and actionable next steps.

Action Step: Frame the conversation around solutions: "What can we do differently to ensure we're aligned moving forward?" Encourage collaborative problem-solving to rebuild trust.

5. Set Clear Agreements

Resolution doesn't end with the conversation—it requires follow-through. Ensure that all parties leave the discussion with clear agreements about behaviors, expectations, and next steps.

Action Step: Summarize the discussion: "Here's what we've agreed on. Let's check in next week to see how things are going and make any adjustments."

Pro Tip: Don't Wait for the Explosion

Most conflicts don't start as full-blown crises—they start as small misunderstandings, miscommunications, or unmet expectations. The longer you wait, the more those small issues grow into big problems. Address them early and often.

How to Spot Conflict Early:

- **Tension in Meetings:** Are people shutting down, talking over each other, or avoiding eye contact?
- **Changes in Behavior:** Is someone more withdrawn, combative, or disengaged than usual?
- **Team Feedback:** Pay attention to side comments or recurring complaints—they're often conflict signals in disguise.

Conflict, when handled well, isn't a liability—it's an **opportunity for growth.** It can clarify expectations, strengthen relationships, and create a more resilient team dynamic. Leaders who address conflict confidently and constructively set the tone for a culture of trust and collaboration.

The Bottom Line: Conflict isn't something to fear—it's something to harness. Lean into it with confidence, and you'll transform potential roadblocks into stepping stones for your team's success.

Continuous Feedback and One on Ones

Feedback and one on ones are essential to connection. When should a leader stop communicating feedback? **Only when they're told to stop.** If connection is the bridge that links a leader to their team, then communication is the foundation that makes that bridge possible. A team can't connect if its members don't feel safe to speak up, share ideas, or raise concerns. Leaders set the tone for this by creating an environment where communication flows freely—up, down, and sideways.

Creating a Feedback-Rich Culture

Here's a leadership truth: **feedback isn't a once-a-year event—it's a daily practice.** The best teams don't wait for annual performance reviews to talk about what's working and what isn't. They give and receive feedback continuously, treating it as a tool for growth rather than a weapon for critique.

How to Build a Feedback-Rich Culture:

1. **Set the Example:** Feedback starts with the leader. Model the behavior by giving feedback that is specific, actionable, and balanced.
    - Example: Instead of saying, "You need to be better at deadlines," say, "I noticed the last project was delayed by two days. Let's talk about how we can better plan timelines moving forward."
2. **Encourage Asking for Feedback:** Feedback is a two-way street. Show your team how to ask for feedback from peers and leaders to make it part of the culture.
    - Example: "What's one thing I could have done better to support you on this project?"
3. **Celebrate Wins:** Feedback isn't just about correcting mistakes—it's about recognizing and reinforcing great work. When leaders highlight achievements, they motivate their teams and show appreciation.
    - Example: "Your presentation was clear, engaging, and well-researched. It really helped move the discussion forward."

Teams that thrive are teams that **talk.** Feedback isn't about finding flaws—it's about helping each other grow, learn, and succeed. It's the difference between a team that stagnates and one that continuously evolves.

Feedback isn't criticism—it's connection. It shows that you care enough to invest in someone's growth. Done right, it strengthens relationships and builds confidence.

The Role of One-on-Ones

While feedback is critical, it's not enough on its own. Regular **one-on-one meetings** provide a structured opportunity to connect with each team member, discuss progress, and address challenges in real time. These conversations foster trust, create alignment, and show your team that you value them as individuals, not just contributors.

Best Practices for One-on-Ones:

1. **Schedule Regularly:** Consistency builds trust. Whether it's weekly or bi-weekly, set a recurring time and stick to it.
   - **Pro Tip:** Block the time on your calendar and treat it as non-negotiable. Canceling sends the message that the conversation isn't a priority.
2. **Focus on the Individual:** Use one-on-ones to discuss more than just tasks. Dive into career aspirations, challenges, and personal development goals.
   - Example: "What skills do you want to develop this year, and how can I help you get there?"
3. **Provide Actionable Feedback:** Feedback during one-on-ones should be specific and tied to actionable improvements.
   - Example: "I noticed that your client reports are thorough but often delivered just before the deadline. Let's explore ways to build in more buffer time."

4. **Review and Reset Goals:** Use these meetings to align on objectives, adjust priorities, and ensure that everyone is focused on the right outcomes.
   - Example: "Let's revisit your goals for Q4. Are they still achievable, or do we need to recalibrate based on recent changes?"
5. **End with a Clear Action Plan:** Each one-on-one should result in clear next steps. Summarize agreements and follow up to ensure accountability.

If connection is the bridge, **continuous and intentional feedback** is the foundational to that bridge. Without open lines of dialogue, teams can't connect, trust falters, and performance suffers. Leaders who prioritize communication through continuous feedback and regular one-on-ones build teams that feel supported, aligned, and empowered.

Helping New Employees Hit the Ground Running

Let's close this chapter by focusing on one of the easiest—and most overlooked—opportunities for leaders to build connection: **onboarding.** Too many leaders miss their first and best chance to connect with new team members during those critical early days, weeks, and even months.

Onboarding isn't just about filling out paperwork or running through checklists; it's about setting the tone for the relationship. This is when new hires form their initial impressions of the organization, their role, and—most importantly—you as their leader. **Get it right, and you create a foundation of trust, engagement, and long-term success.** Miss the mark, and you risk losing their enthusiasm and alignment before they even hit their stride.

Great leaders don't leave onboarding to chance. They treat it as a strategic opportunity to make new hires feel welcomed, valued, and connected—not just to the team but to the organization's vision and mission. This is your moment to set the standard, inspire confidence, and start building the kind of connection that drives lasting results.

Onboarding isn't just an HR function—it's a leadership responsibility. It's the first real chance to demonstrate your commitment to their growth, ensure they feel valued, and integrate them into the team. **The goal isn't just to teach them how to do the job; it's to make them feel like they belong.**

Why Onboarding Matters

Research shows that organizations with a strong onboarding process improve new hire retention by **82%** and productivity by **70%**. Yet, too many leaders treat onboarding as a checklist—a few forms, a quick tour, and a generic welcome email. That's not onboarding; that's neglect.

Effective onboarding does three key things:

1. **Accelerates Connection:** It helps new employees build relationships, not just with their manager but with the entire team.
2. **Sets Expectations:** It provides clarity about their role, goals, and how success will be measured.
3. **Reinforces Culture:** It immerses new hires in the company's values, vision, and unique way of working.

Processes for Successful Onboarding

To help new employees hit the ground running, leaders need to go beyond the basics. Here are practical strategies to create a memorable and effective onboarding experience:

1. Design a Structured Onboarding Process

A haphazard onboarding process sends the wrong message—that you're disorganized or don't prioritize your team. Instead, create a structured plan that covers both the practical and cultural aspects of the role.

What to Include:

- **Role-Specific Training:** Equip them with the tools and knowledge they need to succeed in their specific job.
- **Company Culture Orientation:** Share the company's vision, mission, and values in a way that's inspiring, not just informational.
- **Team Introductions:** Facilitate introductions with team members, including cross-functional peers they'll interact with regularly.
- **First-Week Goals:** Set clear, achievable objectives for their first week to help them build momentum and confidence.

2. Pair Them with a Mentor or Buddy

One of the most impactful ways to ease a new hire's transition is to pair them with someone who's already embedded in the organization —a mentor or buddy.

How It Helps:

- **Navigating Culture:** Mentors can demystify the unwritten rules and norms of the workplace.
- **Building Relationships:** A buddy system provides a friendly face and a go-to person for questions.
- **Encouraging Growth:** Mentors can help new hires identify development opportunities and avoid early pitfalls.

Pro Tip: Choose mentors carefully. They should be high-performing team members who embody the company's values and have a genuine interest in helping others succeed.

3. Schedule Regular Check-Ins

Don't assume everything is fine just because the new hire isn't speaking up. Regular, proactive check-ins are essential to uncover concerns, answer questions, and provide support.

How to Check In Effectively:

- **Weekly for the First Month:** Schedule weekly one-on-ones to discuss their progress, challenges, and questions.
- **Ask Open-Ended Questions:** Create space for honest dialogue. "What's going well? What's been frustrating?"
- **Provide Feedback and Encouragement:** Highlight their wins and offer constructive feedback to keep them on track.

4. Create a Personalized Welcome Experience

The first day sets the tone for everything that follows. A thoughtful, personalized welcome shows that you see your new hire as more than just a name on a roster.

Ideas for a Memorable First Day:

- **Personalized Welcome Kit:** Include branded swag, a handwritten note from the leader, and resources tailored to their role.
- **Team Welcome Video:** Have the team create a short video introducing themselves and sharing why they're excited to work together.
- **Welcome Lunch:** Organize a casual lunch with the team to break the ice and start building relationships.

5. Set Milestones for the First 90 Days

New hires often feel overwhelmed by everything they need to learn and achieve. Break the journey into clear, manageable milestones to give them a sense of progress and accomplishment.

Milestone Examples:

- **Day 30:** Master the basics of their role and complete initial training.
- **Day 60:** Contribute to their first major project or deliverable.
- **Day 90:** Demonstrate independence in their role and outline personal development goals.

6. Foster a Culture of Inclusion

Feeling like part of the team isn't automatic—it's cultivated. Leaders must actively create opportunities for new hires to integrate into the team's culture.

How to Foster Inclusion:

- **Invite Their Perspective:** Ask for their fresh insights on processes or challenges.
- **Encourage Team Bonding:** Plan team-building activities that include new hires, such as brainstorming sessions, offsite events, or casual happy hours.
- **Recognize Their Contributions:** Celebrate their first successes, no matter how small, to reinforce their value to the team.

Onboarding isn't just about helping new hires do their jobs—it's about helping them **belong.** When leaders invest in onboarding, they're not just teaching processes or sharing information; they're building connection, trust, and engagement from day one. Great onboarding is an opportunity to show new hires that they made the right choice. It's your first chance to connect, inspire, and set the stage for their success—and the team's. Don't waste it.

Chapter 4: Key Takeaways

1. Fostering Enthusiasm and Buy-In

Engage team members by involving them in the goal-setting process. When people feel heard and included, they're more enthusiastic, committed, and emotionally invested in achieving the team's vision.

2. Managing Attitudes Proactively

Address negative attitudes before they spiral into larger issues. Approach these situations with empathy and provide constructive, behavior-focused feedback to foster growth and maintain a positive team dynamic.

3. Onboarding with Impact

Set the tone for success from day one. Use structured onboarding processes, mentorship programs, and personalized welcome experiences to help new employees integrate seamlessly, feel valued, and hit the ground running.

4. The Power of Feedback and Communication

Build trust and connection by creating a feedback-rich culture. Maintain open lines of communication through continuous feedback and regular one-on-one meetings to support development, address challenges, and celebrate achievements.

5. Cultivating Connection Intelligence

Turn emotional intelligence into actionable leadership by focusing on the three pillars of connection: teaching, challenging, and role modeling. This approach builds trust, engagement, and a deeper sense of alignment within the team.

6. Transforming Teams into Communities

Create a culture of connection by establishing rituals and traditions that foster belonging and shared purpose. From weekly check-ins to milestone celebrations, these practices help turn individual contributors into a cohesive and resilient community.

Strategies for Implementation

1. **Goal Alignment Workshops**

Conduct interactive workshops where team members align their individual goals with organizational objectives. These sessions not only enhance clarity and focus but also foster a sense of personal investment in shared outcomes.

- **How to Execute:**
  - Begin with a clear presentation of organizational goals and priorities.
  - Facilitate small group discussions to help individuals identify how their work contributes to the larger vision.
  - Use collaborative tools like goal-setting templates to ensure alignment.
- **Bonus:** Conclude the workshop with a "vision map" that visually connects individual contributions to team and organizational success.

2. **Attitude Awareness Programs**

Develop programs aimed at improving workplace attitudes by focusing on communication, empathy, and stress management. These programs proactively address potential attitude problems and reinforce a positive, resilient team culture.

- **How to Execute:**
  - Include role-playing exercises to practice empathy and constructive dialogue in challenging scenarios.
  - Offer training on emotional intelligence, with specific strategies for handling stress and maintaining composure under pressure.

  - Incorporate regular pulse surveys to measure team sentiment and identify areas for improvement.

- **Bonus:** Create a peer-recognition system where team members can acknowledge each other's positive attitudes and contributions.

3. Enhanced Onboarding Kits

Go beyond the basics by creating comprehensive onboarding kits that make new hires feel welcomed, informed, and prepared. These kits should include everything from company culture insights to practical tools for their first year.

- **What to Include:**
  - A personalized welcome letter from leadership.
  - A with fun facts and photos of "team introduction guide" .colleagues
  - A roadmap outlining key milestones for their first 90 days, six months, and year.
  - Access to mentorship opportunities and learning resources.
- **How to Execute:**
  - Pair the onboarding kit with an engaging orientation session that reinforces the company's vision and values.
  - Assign a mentor or buddy to help navigate their early days.
- **Bonus:** Send the kit to the new hire's home before their first day for a personal touch.

4. Feedback Training Sessions

Offer dedicated training sessions that teach team members and leaders how to give and receive feedback effectively. Emphasize the importance of honesty, clarity, and respect to create a culture of trust and continuous improvement.

- **How to Execute:**
  - Use real-world scenarios to practice delivering both positive and constructive feedback.
  - Teach active listening techniques to ensure feedback is received and understood.
  - Provide a framework for structuring feedback, such as the SBI (Situation-Behavior-Impact) model.
- **Bonus:** Incorporate "feedback loops" where participants share how they've applied the feedback they've received, reinforcing accountability and growth.

5. Connection Rituals and Traditions

Establish team rituals and traditions to foster a sense of belonging and transform your team into a thriving community.

- **How to Execute:**
  - Implement weekly check-ins where team members share wins, challenges, and goals.
  - Celebrate milestones—big and small—with personalized recognition or team events.
  - Introduce a monthly "knowledge swap" where team members teach one another skills or share insights.
- **Bonus:** Allow the team to co-create new rituals, ensuring they feel ownership over these practices.

6. Connection Intelligence Development

Train leaders on the three pillars of connection intelligence—teaching, challenging, and role modeling—to create deeper, more meaningful relationships within their teams.

- **How to Execute:**

- Run leadership workshops focused on the practical application of the three pillars.
- Incorporate role-play exercises to practice teaching moments, challenging conversations, and modeling key behaviors.
- Create a peer-coaching program to encourage leaders to hold each other accountable for demonstrating connection intelligence.

- **Bonus:** Share success stories where connection intelligence has driven team performance to reinforce its value.

By enhancing connections within the team through effective communication, empathetic leadership, and supportive practices, leaders can build a more cohesive and motivated workforce.

ROBER LEE BARBER

Chapter 5
COMPLIANCE

"Compliance isn't bureaucracy;
it's the architecture of order and trust."
— Mark Schwartz

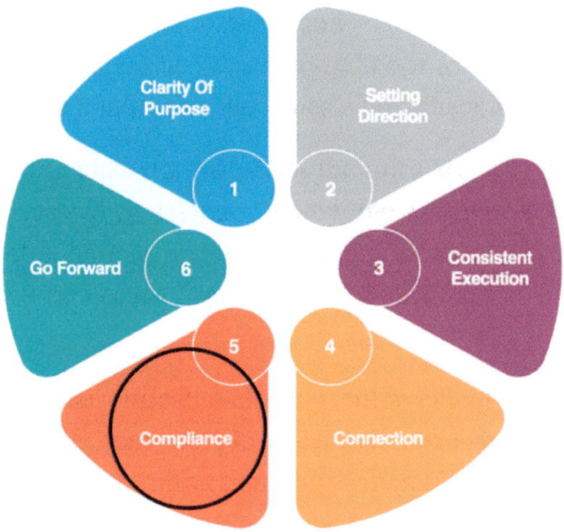

Let's be honest—**compliance doesn't top anyone's list of thrilling leadership topics.** It's rarely flashy, often overlooked, and all too easy to relegate to HR or legal. But here's the thing: **compliance is the backbone of leadership integrity.** It's not about being a bureaucratic buzzkill—it's about creating a foundation of trust, fairness, and accountability that lets teams thrive. Without it, even the most innovative and high-performing organizations can crumble under the weight of scandals, lawsuits, or toxic cultures.

Compliance might not seem exciting, but when done right, it's transformative. It ensures everyone knows the rules of the game, so your team can focus on what really matters—achieving results. Compliance isn't leadership's paperwork; it's leadership's promise.

Why Compliance Matters

Compliance isn't just about keeping the organization out of trouble. It's about creating an environment where people feel safe—safe to do their best work, safe to speak up, and safe to take risks without fear of unfair repercussions. When leaders prioritize compliance, they set the tone for a culture of fairness and integrity.

Imagine a workplace where rules are enforced inconsistently, policies are ignored, and ethics take a backseat to convenience. Chaos doesn't take long to follow. Trust erodes, morale tanks, and people start looking for the nearest exit. Compliance prevents this. It's the guardrail that keeps the organization on track and ensures that trust and fairness remain non-negotiable.

But compliance isn't just about following the rules—it's about understanding **why** those rules exist. They're not obstacles; they're tools. They protect your team, reinforce your values, and ensure that everyone is playing by the same standards.

Playing by the Rules

Every leader operates within a framework of rules—legal, ethical, and organizational. It's not your job to memorize every policy or law, but you need to understand the principles behind them. Ignorance isn't an excuse, and pretending compliance doesn't matter is the fastest way to lose credibility as a leader.

When you encounter gray areas, don't hesitate to consult experts. Build strong relationships with HR, legal counsel, or trusted advisors who can help you navigate complex situations. A single misstep can derail trust, so don't let overconfidence or negligence be your downfall.

And remember: your team watches how you handle compliance. If you cut corners, ignore policies, or tolerate unethical behavior, they'll follow suit. On the flip side, modeling integrity sets the standard for everyone around you.

Building Accountability

Compliance doesn't happen in isolation—it thrives in a culture of accountability. This starts with communication. People are far more likely to respect rules when they understand the reasoning behind them. If you present policies as arbitrary hoops to jump through, don't be surprised when compliance becomes a box-checking exercise.

Leaders must articulate not just **what** the rules are but **why** they exist. For example, instead of saying, "Follow the safety protocol," explain, "This protocol is here to protect you and your team from preventable risks. It's how we ensure everyone goes home safe at the end of the day."

Consistency is also critical. Selective enforcement of rules sends a dangerous message: some people or behaviors are above the standards. Whether it's a minor infraction or a major ethical breach, your response must align with the values you've set for your team.

The Ethical Dimension

Compliance isn't just about legality—it's about ethics. Sometimes, what's legal isn't what's right, and leaders must navigate these gray areas carefully. This is where your moral compass comes into play.

Great leaders consistently ask themselves:

- Is this decision aligned with our values?

- Does it reflect fairness and equity?
- How would this look if it were made public?

Choosing ethics over shortcuts isn't just good leadership—it's good business. Ethical decisions build trust with your team, your customers, and your stakeholders. They show that your organization prioritizes doing what's right over doing what's easy.

Building Trust Through Compliance

Here's the kicker: **compliance done well doesn't feel restrictive—it feels empowering.** When your team knows the boundaries, they can work with confidence, innovate without fear, and focus on achieving results. Compliance provides clarity, and clarity is a powerful enabler of creativity and collaboration.

Teams trust leaders who enforce standards fairly, model integrity, and protect their people from harm. Compliance isn't just about avoiding trouble; it's about showing your team that trust, fairness, and accountability are baked into the way you lead.

Your Role as HR's Partner

As a leader, you're the bridge between HR policies and your team. It's your responsibility to ensure that policies aren't just words on a page but living principles that guide your decisions and actions.

1. Understand Employment Laws and Policies

Ignorance of the law isn't just risky—it's a recipe for disaster. Leaders don't need to be legal experts, but they must understand the fundamentals of employment laws and how these rules impact their teams. From anti-discrimination policies to workplace safety standards, these laws provide a framework for fairness and protection in the workplace.

Why This Matters: Knowing the basics enables you to spot potential red flags, address issues proactively, and prevent costly missteps. It also demonstrates your commitment to creating a workplace where everyone feels valued and protected.

What to Do:

- Take time to familiarize yourself with key policies such as anti-harassment regulations, equal opportunity laws, and health and safety guidelines.
- Attend HR-led training sessions to deepen your understanding of legal and organizational standards.
- Stay informed about updates to employment laws, especially those that directly impact your industry or team.

Pro Tip: If you're ever unsure about how a law or policy applies, don't guess. Reach out to HR early to clarify. It's far better to ask questions upfront than to deal with the consequences of an avoidable mistake later.

2. Communicate Policies Clearly

Policies are only as effective as your team's understanding of them. Handing out an employee handbook is a start, but it's not enough. Leaders must take the time to clearly communicate policies, explain their purpose, and highlight how they benefit the team.

Why This Matters: People are more likely to follow policies when they understand the "why" behind them. Clear communication transforms policies from abstract rules into practical tools that align with the team's goals and values.

What to Do:

- Break down complex policies into simple, relatable terms that your team can easily understand.

- Share real-world examples of how policies support fairness, flexibility, or accountability.
- Use team meetings as an opportunity to reinforce key policies, especially during times of change or when rolling out new initiatives.

Example: If introducing a new remote work policy, explain how it balances flexibility for employees with the need for accountability and collaboration. Share specific expectations, like maintaining availability during core hours or participating in regular check-ins.

3. Actively Support HR Initiatives

HR initiatives—from diversity and inclusion efforts to wellness programs—aren't just corporate buzzwords; they're critical for building a positive and productive workplace. Leaders who champion these initiatives send a powerful message that they care about their team's well-being and success.

Why This Matters: When leaders model participation in HR programs, they set the tone for the entire team. Active support ensures these initiatives are embraced and integrated into the team's culture.

What to Do:

- Be the first to engage with HR programs, whether it's signing up for a wellness workshop or participating in a diversity training session.
- Encourage team members to get involved by highlighting how these initiatives benefit them and the organization.
- Use these programs as opportunities to foster connection, collaboration, and professional growth.

Example: If your company launches a mental health awareness program, sign up for training and openly discuss the importance of mental well-being in team meetings. Share resources and encourage your team to take advantage of the program.

Partnering with HR: A Shared Responsibility

Effective leaders don't treat HR as an afterthought—they see it as a strategic partner in creating a thriving workplace. By understanding policies, communicating them clearly, and championing HR initiatives, you set the tone for a culture of accountability, fairness, and support.

Partnering with HR isn't just about protecting the organization from risks—it's about building an environment where every team member can succeed. When you take ownership of this partnership, you're not just following policies—you're leading with purpose.

Compliance may not be glamorous, but it's the backbone of leadership integrity. It's not about stifling creativity or innovation—it's about creating the trust and clarity that allow both to thrive.

Great leaders don't see compliance as a burden—they see it as an opportunity. An opportunity to set the tone, build trust, and create a culture where accountability and fairness are non-negotiable. When you embrace compliance, you're not just following the rules—you're leading by example.

Handling Tough Situations: Exits and Transitions

Few moments in leadership test your compliance knowledge and emotional intelligence like managing employee exits. Whether it's a resignation, a termination, or a layoff, these situations are inherently sensitive and fraught with legal, emotional, and cultural implications. But here's the harsh reality: **if you're thinking about compliance only when you're preparing to let someone go, it's already too late.**

Compliance Starts Long Before Exits

Most leaders find themselves in hot water not because they lack good intentions but because they've been inconsistent or uninformed about compliance long before an exit becomes inevitable. Terminations and transitions often magnify existing gaps in process, documentation, and fairness. If performance evaluations are inconsistent, feedback has been vague, or policies haven't been enforced, the cracks in your leadership foundation will show.

Being compliant is not something you scramble to achieve in the heat of a difficult situation. It's an ongoing discipline. Documenting performance issues, offering regular feedback, and following organizational protocols consistently aren't just bureaucratic exercises —they're the foundation for respectful, transparent, and defensible decision-making when exits occur.

The Respectful Exit: Why Compliance Matters

When a team member exits, whether voluntarily or involuntarily, **the most respectful thing you can do as a leader is to follow a compliant, fair process.** Compliance isn't just about protecting the organization from lawsuits or reputational harm—it's about treating people with dignity and integrity, even in the most difficult moments.

Think about the message this sends to your remaining team. When employees see that exits are handled fairly, they're more likely to trust leadership, feel secure in their roles, and remain engaged. Mishandling an exit, however, can ripple through the organization, damaging morale and eroding trust.

Key Principles of Respectful Exits:

- **Clarity:** Be transparent about why the exit is occurring and how it aligns with established processes.
- **Consistency:** Ensure that the exit process reflects the same standards applied to others in similar situations.
- **Empathy:** Acknowledge the emotions involved and treat the departing employee as a person, not just a problem to resolve.

Best Practices for Exiting Employees

A compliant, thoughtful approach to exits not only minimizes risk but also strengthens your leadership credibility. Here are best practices to guide the process:

1. **Prepare Thoroughly**
   - **Document Everything:** Ensure that all relevant documentation—performance reviews, disciplinary actions, or exit agreements—is complete, accurate, and readily available.
   - **Follow Company Policies:** Adhere to your organization's termination or resignation procedures, including notice periods, severance terms, and final paycheck requirements.
2. **Communicate Clearly**
   - **Be Direct, Yet Compassionate:** When informing an employee about their exit, clarity is critical. Be honest about the reasons and next steps, but do so with respect and empathy.
   - **Plan the Conversation:** Prepare talking points in advance to ensure you stay on track and cover all necessary details.
3. **Ensure Professionalism**
   - **Maintain Confidentiality:** Share information about the exit on a need-to-know basis to protect the employee's privacy.
   - **Stay Neutral:** Avoid personal judgments or emotional reactions, even if the situation is contentious.
4. **Conduct Exit Interviews**
   - **Make It Meaningful:** Use exit interviews to gather honest feedback about your organization, team dynamics, or leadership practices.
   - **Ask Open-Ended Questions:** Encourage departing employees to share insights without fear of repercussion. For example:

   - "What do you think we could have done differently to support you better?"
   - "What advice would you give to improve this role for future team members?"

5. **Support Transitions**
   - **Provide Resources:** Offer guidance on benefits, severance, or outplacement services where applicable.
   - **Focus on Closure:** End the process with gratitude for their contributions and a clear explanation of what comes next.

How you handle exits isn't just a reflection of your leadership—it's a statement about your organization's values. Leaders who prioritize compliance and respect in these moments signal to their teams that integrity is non-negotiable, even in challenging circumstances.

The truth is, people may not remember every detail of their employment, but they will remember how they were treated on their way out. When you approach exits with fairness, empathy, and professionalism, you're not just protecting your organization—you're building a culture where accountability and respect are the norm.

And here's the kicker: doing exits well isn't just about the individual leaving—it's about the people staying. Every exit is an opportunity to reinforce trust, strengthen morale, and demonstrate that leadership is as much about doing what's right as it is about driving results.

Play by the rules. Protect your team. Watch your leadership soar.

Chapter 5 : Key Takeaways

1. Compliance as a Leadership Foundation

Compliance is more than paperwork; it's the foundation of integrity, trust, and accountability in leadership. It ensures clarity, fairness, and a safe environment where teams can thrive.

2. The Power of Ethics

Compliance isn't just about legality—it's about doing what's right. Ethical decisions build trust with your team, customers, and stakeholders, reinforcing your commitment to values over shortcuts.

3. Accountability Drives Compliance

Building a culture of accountability ensures everyone takes responsibility for upholding standards. Consistent enforcement and clear communication of policies foster trust and respect.

4. Handling Exits with Respect

Managing employee transitions with professionalism and empathy not only safeguards the organization's integrity but also maintains team morale and trust.

5. Leaders as HR Partners

Effective leaders bridge the gap between HR policies and team execution. Understanding and enforcing employment laws, supporting HR initiatives, and promoting fairness are critical components of leadership.

Strategies for Implementation

1. Compliance and Ethics Training Sessions

Regularly conduct workshops for leaders and team members to ensure they understand the principles behind compliance and ethical decision-making.

- Focus on real-world scenarios to make the training practical and relatable.
- Include interactive discussions about gray areas and how to navigate them.

2. Clear and Accessible Policy Communication

Make HR policies and compliance guidelines easy to access and understand.

- Create visual summaries or FAQs for complex policies to improve clarity.
- Host quarterly Q&A sessions to address common questions and concerns.

3. Accountability Frameworks

Establish systems that reinforce accountability across all levels of the organization.

- Use team meetings to discuss the importance of compliance and share examples of ethical leadership.
- Implement a system for anonymous reporting of compliance concerns to foster transparency.

4. Proactive Partnership with HR

Strengthen the connection between leadership and HR to support compliance efforts.

- Schedule regular check-ins with HR to stay updated on policies and legal requirements.
- Collaborate on initiatives like diversity programs, employee wellness, and inclusion efforts.

5. Exit Process Book

Develop a standardized process for managing employee exits that prioritizes compliance and respect.

- Include checklists to ensure all legal and procedural requirements are met.
- Train leaders on how to conduct respectful and constructive exit interviews.

6. Ethical Leadership as a Core Competency

Embed ethics into your leadership development programs.

- Create leadership workshops that focus on aligning decisions with organizational values.
- Reward and recognize leaders who exemplify ethical behavior in challenging situations.

By understanding and actively participating in these compliance-related areas, leaders not only protect the organization from legal risks but also contribute to a work environment that is fair, respectful, and supportive of all employees. This proactive approach to compliance reinforces the organization's commitment to ethical practices and employee well-being.

Chapter 6
GOING FORWARD

"The best way to predict the future is to create it."
— Peter Drucker

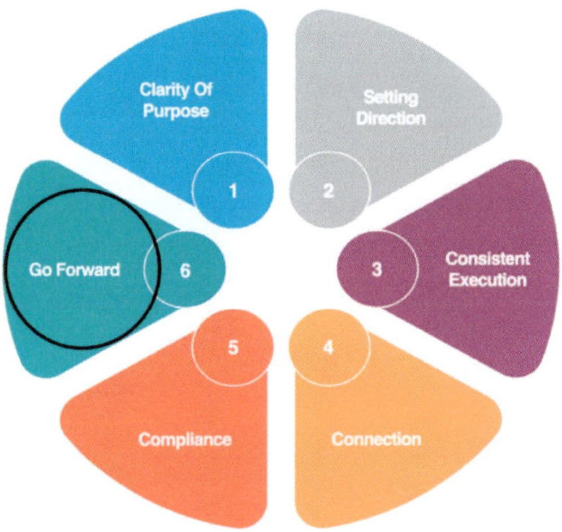

We've reached the final quadrant of the Leading by Design Operating Model, but don't mistake this for the finish line. **Go Forward Development** isn't about concluding your journey—it's about continuing it. This component emphasizes the truth that leadership is never static; it's a living, evolving process. It's the part of the model that ensures leaders don't just manage for today but build for tomorrow.

A quick note on the nomenclature: **Go Forward Development** signifies not only the importance of a leader's role in developing themselves and their people but also underscores the cyclical nature of the Leading by Design model. The process is designed to be repeatable, moving seamlessly from one quadrant to the next, reinforcing growth and progress at every step.

Leadership, at its best, isn't just about solving the problems right in front of you—it's about anticipating the challenges ahead and preparing yourself and your team to face them. As the Peter Drucker quote opens this chapter heading, it is best to predict the future by creating it. Go Forward Development is the engine of growth for the leader and the team. It's where the daily grind transforms into a legacy, where personal and team development are prioritized not as afterthoughts but as essential, ongoing practices. This quadrant is the difference between leaders who tread water and those who create ripples that last long after they're gone.

Leadership as a Growth Process

Here's the reality: **if you're not growing, you're falling behind.** Leadership isn't a skill you learn once and apply forever. It's an evolving practice that demands continuous learning and adaptation. Great leaders are like sponges—they soak up knowledge from books, conferences, mentors, and, most importantly, their own teams. They don't just seek feedback—they embrace it, knowing that every critique is a chance to improve.

But here's the key: **growth isn't just for you—it's for your team too.** Leaders who prioritize their team's development build more than just high-performing groups; they build loyalty, engagement, and trust. When your people see that you're invested in their future, they'll invest in your vision.

For growth to be meaningful, it needs to be intentional. It's not about checking boxes; it's about crafting opportunities. Encourage your team to take on stretch projects, support them in developing new skills, and challenge them to think beyond their current roles. Growth isn't comfortable, but it's necessary, and great leaders don't just push their teams—they grow alongside them.

Mentorship: Multiplying Your Impact

Leadership isn't about doing everything yourself—it's about multiplying your impact through others. That's where mentorship comes in. Mentorship is one of the most powerful tools a leader has, not just for developing their team but for sharpening their own leadership skills.

Think of mentorship as an investment in exponential growth. It's about transferring knowledge, sharing lessons learned, and helping others navigate challenges you've already faced. But mentorship isn't about dictating solutions—it's about guiding your mentees to find their own. Great mentors don't just tell people what to do; they teach them how to think.

Here's the beauty of mentorship: it's not a one-way street. Every time you mentor someone, you gain as much as you give. Teaching forces you to clarify your own ideas, reflect on your experiences, and evolve as a leader. And let's be honest—there's nothing more satisfying than watching someone you've mentored rise to new heights.

Ensuring Mentorship for Everyone

But mentorship isn't just an optional perk for a few top performers—it's a non-negotiable for every member of your team. Yes, everyone. As a leader, your role in the Leading by Design model isn't just to mentor directly but to ensure that mentorship exists as a cornerstone of your team's culture.

Why does this matter? Because mentorship fuels growth, engagement, and retention. A team where everyone has a mentor is a team where people feel supported, challenged, and connected. It's where individual potential is unlocked, and collective performance soars.

How to Build a Mentorship-Driven Culture:

1. **Pair Every Team Member with a Mentor:** Whether it's a peer mentor, a senior leader, or even someone outside the organization, ensure that every team member has access to guidance and support tailored to their goals.

2. **Set Clear Expectations:** Define the purpose and goals of mentorship relationships. This might include skill development, career planning, or navigating specific challenges.

3. **Provide Mentorship Training:** Not everyone instinctively knows how to be a good mentor. Offer training to help mentors ask better questions, listen actively, and empower their mentees.

4. **Make It Measurable:** Regularly check in on mentorship relationships to ensure they're delivering value to both parties. Ask questions like: What's working? What progress has been made? What challenges remain?

5. **Lead by Example:** Be an active mentor yourself. Show your team that mentorship isn't just something you promote—it's something you practice.

The Ripple Effect of Mentorship

When you create a culture where mentorship is universal, you unlock a ripple effect of growth and impact. Team members who are mentored become mentors themselves, cascading knowledge and support throughout the organization.

And mentorship isn't limited to skill-building; it's also about fostering connection. A strong mentorship culture strengthens bonds, builds trust, and reinforces a shared sense of purpose. It creates an environment where people feel invested in each other's success, driving both individual and team performance.

In the end, mentorship isn't just a leadership tool—it's a leadership responsibility. By ensuring that everyone on your team has a mentor, you're not just multiplying your impact—you're creating a legacy of growth, support, and excellence that will extend far beyond your tenure.

Succession Planning: Leadership That Lasts

If your organization or team falls apart without you, you haven't led—you've babysat. True leadership isn't about being indispensable; it's about creating systems, developing people, and building structures that can thrive without you. And here's another truth: this principle applies no matter the size of your team. Whether you lead a handful of people or a sprawling organization, succession planning is not optional—it's essential.

Succession planning isn't something to put off until you lose a key team member. Waiting for someone to walk out the door—or worse, being caught off guard by their departure—is a recipe for chaos. Great leaders don't just react to turnover; they anticipate it. They plan for it. Succession planning is the ultimate test of leadership because it ensures your team's success continues long after you've moved on.

The reluctance to embrace succession planning often comes from fear—it feels like planning your own obsolescence. But here's the mindset shift: succession planning isn't about making yourself irrelevant; it's about ensuring your impact endures. It's about building a legacy of resilience and capability that reflects your leadership long after your tenure.

And let's make it personal: **Who is your replacement?** If you left tomorrow, who could step into your shoes? If you don't know the answer—or if the answer makes you uneasy—it's time to focus on developing your successor. Great leaders don't avoid this question;

they lean into it. They see growing their replacement not as a threat but as the ultimate validation of their leadership.

How to Embed Succession Planning into Your Leadership DNA

1. Identify High-Potential Team Members

Look for more than just high performance in current roles. Seek out individuals who demonstrate curiosity, adaptability, and a hunger to grow. These are the people who have the capacity to step into larger roles and take on greater challenges.

Pro Tip: Don't overlook emerging talent just because they're new or less experienced. Sometimes, the best leaders of tomorrow are the ones asking the right questions today.

2. Develop Your Replacement

You can't just hope the right person will emerge when you leave—you need to actively cultivate them. Identify someone on your team who has the potential to take your role and invest in their growth.

How to Do It:

- Give them visibility: Involve them in high-level meetings and decision-making processes.
- Share knowledge: Regularly debrief with them on how and why you make leadership decisions.
- Assign responsibility: Let them take ownership of projects or initiatives you would normally handle.

Ask Yourself: What are you doing today to prepare your replacement for tomorrow?

3. Develop Their Skills Through Stretch Assignments

Give your team members opportunities to grow beyond their current responsibilities. Assign stretch projects that challenge them to think strategically, solve complex problems, or lead cross-functional efforts.

Example: If you have someone excelling in operations, let them take on a strategic planning initiative. If a team member shines in technical expertise, give them a chance to lead a project and manage a team.

4. Involve Them in Strategic Decisions

Succession planning isn't just about tasks; it's about mindset. Include high-potential team members in strategic conversations so they can see the big picture and understand the organization's long-term goals.

Pro Tip: Shadowing senior leaders or being part of decision-making committees gives your team members invaluable insight into what leadership entails.

5. Create a Culture of Leadership Development

Succession planning isn't a one-time event—it's a continuous process. Make leadership development a part of your team's culture by encouraging ongoing learning, mentoring, and cross-training.

Example: Rotate responsibilities among team members to give everyone a chance to learn new skills and experience different aspects of the business.

6. Align Succession Planning with Team and Organizational Goals

Succession planning isn't just about filling vacancies—it's about aligning talent development with the broader vision. When your team understands that their growth is tied to the success of the organization, they're more likely to buy into the process.

Pro Tip: Communicate the "why" behind succession planning. It's not just about preparing for someone's departure—it's about ensuring the team's stability and growth.

When leaders embrace succession planning, they ensure their teams aren't just surviving but thriving—regardless of who's at the helm. And no matter how small your team is, the principles remain the same.

Succession planning builds trust. It signals to your team that you're not just focused on today's results but also on their long-term development and the organization's future success. It creates a culture of resilience, where transitions are smooth, and opportunities for growth are celebrated, not feared.

Grooming Your Replacement: Developing your successor isn't a sign of weakness—it's a sign of strength. It shows that you care about the team's success more than your ego. It ensures that your hard work, vision, and leadership endure long after you're gone.

Leadership isn't about being the one who always saves the day. It's about creating an environment where your team can save the day—with or without you. That's not a sign of irrelevance—it's the mark of an extraordinary leader.

Feedback: The Catalyst for Growth

We have already touched on continuous feedback, but just to touch on again, feedback is also the lifeblood of Go Forward Development. Without it, growth stagnates, blind spots go unnoticed, and opportunities for improvement are lost. Great leaders don't wait for annual reviews to provide feedback—they make it a continuous part of their leadership style.

But feedback isn't just about pointing out mistakes. Constructive feedback helps your team learn and improve, while positive feedback reinforces the behaviors you want to see more of. And remember: **feedback is a two-way street.** Asking for feedback from your team, peers, and mentors keeps you grounded and sharp.

Feedback is also an opportunity to build trust. When you provide it with honesty and empathy, you show your team that you care about their growth. When you ask for it with humility, you demonstrate that you're willing to grow alongside them.

Building a Culture of Development

Development isn't just an individual pursuit—it's a team culture. Teams that prioritize learning and growth don't just survive—they thrive. They adapt to change, embrace challenges, and innovate fearlessly.

Creating a culture of development starts with you. Celebrate learning, not just success. Encourage risks and frame failures as opportunities to improve. Normalize mentorship so that everyone has the chance to teach and learn from each other. When growth becomes a team value, it creates an environment where progress feels natural and inevitable.

The 9-Box Grid: Tool for Go Forward Development

When it comes to evaluating and planning for team development, the **9-Box Grid** is one of the most powerful tools at a leader's disposal. Originally designed for talent management and succession planning, the 9-Box is a simple yet effective framework for assessing team members based on two critical dimensions: **performance** and **potential**.

Why the 9-Box Matters

The beauty of the 9-Box Grid lies in its ability to provide clarity. It's easy to see who's excelling, who's struggling, and who has the potential to take on more responsibility. More importantly, it forces leaders to think critically and strategically about their team, moving beyond gut feelings or generic performance reviews.

How It Works

The grid is divided into nine squares, with performance on one axis and potential on the other. Each team member is mapped onto the grid based on where they fall:

- **High Performers with High Potential:** These are your future leaders—the ones you need to groom for bigger roles.
- **High Performers with Moderate Potential:** Solid contributors who may not aspire to leadership but are critical to the team's success.
- **Low Performers with High Potential:** These team members have untapped potential but need guidance, support, or motivation to thrive.

How to Use the 9-Box in Go Forward Development

1. **Assess Objectively:** Use data and specific examples to plot team members accurately. Avoid bias or favoritism.
2. **Develop Action Plans:** For each category, create tailored development strategies.
    - High Performers with High Potential: Provide stretch assignments, mentorship opportunities, and leadership training.
    - Moderate Performers with Moderate Potential: Focus on skill-building and targeted feedback to help them progress.
    - Low Performers: Identify root causes and address barriers to improvement.
3. **Revisit Regularly:** The 9-Box isn't a one-time exercise. Reassess team members quarterly or biannually to track progress and adjust strategies.

The 9-Box Grid isn't just a chart—it's a dynamic tool that drives intentional development. It ensures leaders invest time and resources where they'll have the greatest impact, creating a pipeline of talent that's ready for future challenges.

The Necessity of Development Planning

Let's face it: development planning is often treated as an afterthought —a "nice-to-have" that leaders get to when everything else is done. But here's the reality: **development planning isn't optional—it's essential.** It's how you future-proof your team, retain top talent, and ensure continuous growth.

Why Development Planning Matters

Without a clear plan, growth becomes random and inconsistent. Team members can feel lost, disengaged, or undervalued. Worse, they may stagnate, leaving both their potential and your team's effectiveness on the table. Development planning isn't just about skill-building; it's about creating a roadmap for progress and ensuring everyone feels invested in their growth.

One-on-Ones: The Power of Personalized Planning

We have touched on one on ones as well previously, but lets get a little more detail as it relates to development planning. Often one on ones are just left to giving feedback on why someone stinks at their job or giving over to do lists. One-on-ones are the perfect setting for individualized development planning. These conversations provide a safe, focused space to discuss aspirations, challenges, and growth opportunities.

How to Integrate Development Planning into One-on-Ones:

1. **Start with Goals:** Ask team members about their short- and long-term goals. What do they want to achieve in the next 6 months? In the next 5 years?

2. **Identify Gaps:** Work together to pinpoint the skills or experiences they need to reach those goals.

3. **Create Actionable Steps:** Break big goals into smaller, achievable actions. For example, "Improve leadership skills" becomes "Take the lead on one team project this quarter."

4. **Follow Up:** Revisit the development plan regularly to track progress, adjust as needed, and celebrate milestones.

Why This Works:

When leaders prioritize development in one-on-ones, it sends a powerful message: "Your growth matters to me." This not only boosts engagement but also builds trust and loyalty.

Development Planning in Group Settings

While one-on-ones are critical for personal development, group settings are equally important for fostering team growth and alignment. Team-wide development planning creates opportunities for collaboration, shared learning, and collective progress.

How to Approach Development Planning in Groups:

1. **Team Skills Assessment:** Start by identifying the skills your team as a whole needs to succeed. This might include technical expertise, communication, or problem-solving.

2. **Set Collective Goals:** Align the team around shared objectives that contribute to both individual growth and organizational success.

3. **Leverage Peer Learning:** Encourage team members to teach each other. For example, someone skilled in data analysis could lead a workshop for colleagues who want to improve in that area.

4. **Celebrate Progress Together:** Recognize team milestones and achievements to reinforce the importance of growth.

Unique Ideas for Group Development Planning:

- **Learning Sprints:** Dedicate one week each quarter to a specific skill or topic, with team members sharing insights or resources they've discovered.
- **Collaborative Projects:** Assign cross-functional projects that challenge team members to step outside their comfort zones and learn from one another.
- **Development Retreats:** Host a day-long or weekend retreat focused on skill-building, strategic planning, and team bonding.

Why Group Development Planning Matters

When done well, team development planning builds cohesion and strengthens the collective muscle of the group. It ensures that growth isn't siloed to individuals but shared as a team value.

Bringing It All Together

Development planning—whether done one-on-one or in a group setting—isn't a "nice-to-have"; it's the backbone of Go Forward Development. It's how leaders ensure their teams are prepared for the challenges of tomorrow while staying engaged and motivated today.

Growth doesn't just happen—it's planned. Leaders who prioritize development create teams that don't just perform but thrive. Whether it's through the 9-Box Grid, personalized one-on-ones, or collaborative group initiatives, the goal is the same: to build a future-ready team that can tackle anything.

Chapter 6: Key Takeaways

1. **Growth is Non-Negotiable:** Commit to ongoing personal and team development as a cornerstone of effective leadership.

2. **Mentorship Multiplies Impact:** Use mentorship to expand your influence and create lasting relationships that drive mutual growth.
3. **Succession Planning is Leadership:** Future-proof your organization by identifying and developing the next generation of leaders.
4. **Feedback Fuels Development:** Make feedback a constant and constructive part of your leadership style to foster growth and improvement.
5. **Culture is Key:** Build a team culture that prioritizes learning, risk-taking, and mentorship as core values.

Processes for Implementation

1. **Leadership Development Plans:** Create structured development plans for yourself and your team, aligned with organizational goals and tailored to individual growth needs.
2. **Mentorship Frameworks:** Establish mentorship programs that pair experienced leaders with emerging talent, fostering mutual growth and succession readiness.
3. **Regular Feedback Mechanisms:** Implement tools and routines for continuous feedback, such as weekly check-ins, project debriefs, and peer reviews.
4. **Quarterly Learning Initiatives:** Dedicate one day each quarter to team-wide learning—workshops, book discussions, or skill-building sessions.
5. **Succession Roadmaps:** Identify high-potential talent and design clear pathways for their development, including stretch assignments and leadership shadowing opportunities.

By prioritizing these strategies, leaders can ensure that they and their teams are not only prepared for the challenges of today but are also developing the skills and knowledge necessary to meet the demands of the future. This proactive approach to leadership development fosters a resilient, adaptable, and forward-thinking team.

CLOSING

Reflecting on the Journey

Congratulations—you've made it. Not just to the end of this book, but to the starting line of something bigger. If you've worked through the **Leading by Design Operating Model**, you've already done something that separates leaders from managers: you've chosen to lead with intention. That's no small feat.

Here's the thing about leadership—it's not about getting it right all the time. Perfection is a myth that too many leaders chase and fail to catch. Leadership isn't measured in perfect decisions or spotless execution; it's measured in impact, growth, and the ability to inspire others to do the same. It's about showing up every day, willing to learn, willing to adapt, and willing to lead.

This closing chapter isn't a finish line. If you're looking for a gold star or a pat on the back, you've missed the point. What you hold in your hands isn't a manual for getting leadership "done." It's a framework for starting—and continuing—the work that never ends. Leadership is messy, relentless, and deeply rewarding. The **Leading by Design Operating Model** is your compass, but it's not the journey itself. **Action is the map.**

Now comes the hard part: taking what you've learned here and putting it to work. Because knowing and doing are two entirely different beasts. Every principle, every quadrant, every strategy laid out in this model means nothing if it stays on these pages. The real magic happens when you bring this model to life in your team, your organization, and yourself.

Leadership isn't a destination. You'll never "arrive," and that's the point. It's a journey that demands curiosity, resilience, and a commitment to constant growth. And let me tell you, the view from this road—when you're leading with clarity, purpose, and intention—is extraordinary.

So here's the question: Are you ready to stop reading and start leading? Because everything you've learned here has one purpose—to make you not just a better leader, but a leader who makes others better. That's the challenge. That's the opportunity. And that's where this journey really begins.

Revisiting the Six Quadrants

Let's take a moment to step back and look at the full picture. The **Leading by Design Operating Model** isn't a collection of disconnected concepts—it's a system, a cohesive framework where each quadrant reinforces the others. Mastering one quadrant is good. Mastering all six? That's transformational.

- **Clarity of Purpose** is where it all begins. Without clarity, leadership is aimless. This quadrant aligns your personal vision with the organization's vision, providing the foundation for every decision, action, and strategy that follows. It's the "why" behind everything you do as a leader.

- **Setting Direction** turns that vision into reality. It's the bridge between dreaming and doing, translating big ideas into actionable goals that your team can rally behind. This is where alignment happens—where everyone pulls in the same direction toward shared outcomes.

- **Consistent Execution** is what separates leaders who talk from leaders who deliver. Prioritization, time management, and follow-through aren't just tasks; they're the engine that keeps your leadership running. Execution isn't glamorous, but it's essential—without it, even the best plans collapse.

- **Connection** is the glue. Leadership isn't just about tasks and metrics—it's about people. This quadrant is where trust, collaboration, and engagement come to life. It's how you turn a group of individuals into a team, and a team into a community.

- **Compliance** provides the guardrails. It's not the most exciting quadrant, but it's the one that ensures fairness, integrity, and accountability. Compliance isn't just about following the rules—it's about creating a culture where trust can thrive and where your leadership stands on solid ground.

- **Go Forward Development** is the long game. Leadership isn't just about solving today's problems—it's about preparing for tomorrow's challenges. Growth, mentorship, and succession planning aren't luxuries; they're necessities. This quadrant ensures that your impact lasts far beyond your tenure.

These quadrants don't exist in isolation—they're deeply interconnected. Clarity of Purpose drives Setting Direction, which relies on Consistent Execution to succeed. Connection amplifies all of them, ensuring that your team isn't just working—they're working together. Compliance creates the trust and integrity that underpin every decision, and Go Forward Development ensures that the entire system evolves and grows over time.

Mastering this framework isn't about perfection. It's about understanding how these elements work together and leaning into the areas where you and your team need to grow. **The power of the Leading by Design model lies in its wholeness.** It's not a checklist; it's a way of thinking, leading, and building something bigger than yourself.

So here's the challenge: as you reflect on these six quadrants, ask yourself not just how far you've come, but where you'll go next. Because leadership isn't static, and neither is this model. It grows with you, evolving as you do. And that's the point—it's designed not just to guide you, but to empower you to design your own path forward.

The Role of Intentional Leadership

Leadership, at its core, is a choice—a choice to lead with purpose instead of drifting through the chaos of circumstances. It's about taking control, steering the ship, and refusing to let the winds of the moment dictate your direction. **Intentional leadership** isn't about reacting; it's about anticipating, aligning, and acting with clarity and conviction.

Here's the reality: most people are stuck in reactive mode. They manage their days by putting out fires, responding to noise, and hoping the important stuff doesn't slip through the cracks. But great leaders—the ones who inspire, grow, and transform organizations—operate differently. They choose to lead with intention.

The **Leading by Design Operating Model** is your book for intentionality. It equips you with a system to lead proactively, strategically, and with impact. This isn't about being a hero who works harder or longer—it's about being a leader who works smarter, aligning every action with a clear purpose and a long-term vision.

Leading with Purpose

At the heart of intentional leadership is purpose. Clarity of Purpose, the first quadrant of this model, is where it all starts. Without a deep understanding of your "why," leadership becomes aimless. Intentional leaders don't just know their purpose—they communicate it, live it, and align their teams around it. Purpose is the anchor that keeps you steady when circumstances try to pull you off course.

Moving from Reactive to Proactive

The power of the **Leading by Design model** lies in its ability to move leaders from reacting to leading. Each quadrant pushes you toward intentionality:

- **Setting Direction** ensures that your team isn't guessing—they're aligned around actionable goals.

- **Consistent Execution** helps you build systems and momentum to turn plans into outcomes.
- **Connection** reminds you that leadership isn't about tasks; it's about people and the relationships that drive results.
- **Compliance** ensures you're leading with integrity, providing the guardrails that keep you and your team grounded.
- **Go Forward Development** challenges you to think beyond today and build for the future.

When you approach leadership through these lenses, you stop reacting to what's urgent and start focusing on what's important. You become a leader with a plan, a purpose, and a path forward.

The Importance of Self-Actualization

Intentional leadership begins with knowing yourself. What are your strengths? Your blind spots? Your triggers? Leaders who lack self-awareness are like drivers who refuse to look at the map—they might be moving fast, but they're not necessarily moving in the right direction.

This model challenges you to grow, not just as a leader of others, but as a leader of yourself. It requires reflection, humility, and the courage to admit when you're wrong. Because let's face it: leadership is messy, and even the best leaders stumble. The difference is that intentional leaders learn, adapt, and grow from those stumbles.

Alignment as a Leadership Superpower

Sustainable leadership isn't about individual heroics—it's about alignment. When your purpose, vision, and actions are aligned, leadership becomes fluid. The same is true for your team. Aligned teams don't just work harder—they work smarter, with clarity and confidence in their direction.

The **Leading by Design Operating Model** is designed to help you build that alignment. It's a system that ties your actions to your purpose, your team's efforts to your vision, and your decisions to your values. When alignment is present, leadership stops feeling like a grind and starts feeling like a flow.

Leadership as a Choice

Leadership by design isn't something that happens to you—it's something you choose every day. It's the decision to be purposeful instead of reactive, strategic instead of scattered, and proactive instead of passive. It's the commitment to lead with clarity, accountability, and intention, no matter the challenges you face.

The beauty of this model is that it gives you the tools to make those choices easier. It's not about perfection—it's about progress. It's about deciding, every day, to show up and lead with purpose.

So, as you prepare to step out of this book and into the real world of leadership, ask yourself: **What kind of leader do you want to be?** The reactive one who lets circumstances dictate their path? Or the intentional one who leads with clarity, purpose, and impact? The choice is yours—and it's a choice you'll make every day.

The Legacy of Leadership

Let's talk about legacy. The kind of leadership that doesn't just check boxes or hit quarterly targets but leaves an indelible mark on the people, the culture, and the organization you serve. Great leaders don't measure success by what they achieve during their tenure—they measure it by what endures after they're gone. **Your legacy isn't about you; it's about the impact you've created.**

Leadership that focuses only on the present might feel productive, but it's ultimately shortsighted. Sure, you can drive results today, but what happens when you're not in the room? Does the team crumble? Does the culture falter? If so, you haven't led—you've merely managed.

Leadership Beyond Metrics

Legacy is about the people you've inspired, the leaders you've developed, and the culture you've nurtured. It's reflected in how your team operates without you, in the way they carry forward the principles and practices you've instilled.

Developing Others: Your legacy is directly tied to the growth of the people you lead. Did you mentor someone into their first leadership role? Did you give stretch opportunities that helped your team members achieve what they didn't think was possible? Developing others is the ultimate multiplier for leadership impact.

Building Resilient Teams: Resilient teams are self-sustaining. They don't need constant oversight because they've been equipped with the tools, trust, and autonomy to thrive. This resilience doesn't happen by accident—it's the result of intentional leadership that focuses on empowerment over micromanagement.

Creating a Lasting Culture: Culture is the soul of an organization. Leaders who shape positive, values-driven cultures leave behind something far greater than any single project or achievement. Culture outlasts titles, tenures, and even crises—it's the glue that holds everything together.

What Will You Leave Behind?

As you reflect on the **Leading by Design Operating Model**, think about how each quadrant contributes to your legacy:

- **Clarity of Purpose** ensures that your leadership is grounded in vision and values, giving your team a clear direction to follow long after you're gone.
- **Setting Direction** creates actionable goals that don't just drive results—they set the standard for how to align efforts toward shared success.

- **Consistent Execution** instills the habits and systems that ensure progress continues even without constant intervention.
- **Connection** builds trust and engagement, fostering a sense of belonging that endures beyond any one leader.
- **Compliance** creates a foundation of integrity and accountability that strengthens the organization from the inside out.
- **Go Forward Development** future-proofs your leadership, ensuring that the next generation is prepared to carry the torch.

Your legacy isn't built in the big moments—it's built in the day-to-day. It's in how you handle conflict, how you celebrate wins, how you guide your team through challenges, and how you invest in their growth.

A Call to Reflect

Take a moment to ask yourself: **What kind of leader do I want to be remembered as?** What impact do you want to leave on the people who've worked alongside you? What principles do you want to embed in your team's culture? These aren't abstract questions—they're the foundation of your leadership journey.

Legacy isn't about ego—it's about responsibility. It's about knowing that your leadership doesn't exist in a vacuum and that the choices you make today will ripple far into the future. Great leaders don't just lead for themselves—they lead for others, for their teams, for the vision, and for the values they stand for.

At the end of the day, leadership isn't about what you accomplished—it's about what you set in motion. The best leaders don't just build teams; they build communities. They don't just solve problems; they inspire solutions. They don't just manage for the present; they prepare for the future.

Leadership by design is leadership that lasts. It's leadership that ensures the people, the culture, and the vision you've nurtured will thrive long after you've moved on. That's the legacy you're building, one decision, one conversation, one action at a time.

So, what will your legacy be? The answer is yours to create.

Implementing the Model: Taking the First Steps

You've made it through the framework, absorbed the principles, and reflected on what leadership by design truly means. Now comes the most important part: **putting it into action.** Because leadership isn't what you know—it's what you do.

Here's the reality: implementing the **Leading by Design Operating Model** isn't about flipping a switch. It's a process, one that requires focus, intentionality, and the patience to grow over time. The good news? You don't have to do it all at once. Leadership is about progress, not perfection.

Step 1: Conduct a Self-Assessment

Start by looking in the mirror—not with judgment, but with curiosity. Ask yourself:

- Which quadrants are my strengths? Where do I naturally excel?
- Which quadrants need work? Where do I feel stretched, uncertain, or ineffective?

Be honest. Great leaders aren't afraid to confront their blind spots because they know self-awareness is the foundation of growth. Maybe you're great at Setting Direction but struggle with Connection. Or perhaps Compliance feels like second nature, but Go Forward Development leaves you feeling uncertain. The goal isn't to fix everything overnight; it's to identify where you can start.

Step 2: Choose One Quadrant to Focus On

Leadership is overwhelming when you try to tackle everything at once. That's why the key to implementing this model is focus. Choose one quadrant to prioritize for the next 90 days.

For example:

- If **Connection** is your focus, set a goal to build trust through regular one-on-ones or team-building initiatives.
- If **Consistent Execution** needs work, start with prioritization tools like the Eisenhower Matrix or time-blocking techniques.
- If **Go Forward Development** is your weak spot, commit to mentoring one high-potential team member or creating a succession plan.

By narrowing your focus, you give yourself the bandwidth to make meaningful progress without feeling overwhelmed.

Step 3: Involve Your Team

Leadership isn't a solo act. If you want the **Leading by Design Operating Model** to truly take root, bring your team into the process. Share the framework with them—be transparent about what you're working on and invite their input.

Here's why this matters:

- **Collaboration Builds Buy-In:** When your team feels involved, they're more likely to support the changes you're implementing.
- **Perspective Brings Clarity:** Your team can offer insights into your leadership that you might not see yourself.
- **Accountability Drives Progress:** Sharing your goals publicly keeps you motivated to follow through.

For example, you might say, "I've been reflecting on how I can improve as a leader, and I want to focus on building stronger connections within our team. I'd love your feedback on how I can better support and engage you moving forward."

Step 4: Start Small, Stay Consistent

The biggest mistake leaders make when trying to implement change is biting off more than they can chew. They try to overhaul everything at once, only to burn out or lose momentum. Don't fall into that trap.

Start with small, consistent actions that align with your chosen quadrant. For instance:

- If you're focusing on **Setting Direction**, schedule a weekly strategy meeting to align your team on goals.
- If **Compliance** is your priority, commit to reviewing one policy or process each week to ensure it aligns with your values.

Small wins build momentum. And momentum, over time, leads to transformation.

Applying the Leading by Design Model to Lead Every Day

One of my biggest pet peeves—and a personal promise I made when transitioning into coaching and consulting—was to never take on a project or assignment without crystal-clear objectives, defined measurements, and absolute clarity on how success would be applied and evaluated. So, let's talk application.

Leadership isn't a one-time event or a title—it's a daily practice. It's about showing up with intention, clarity, and consistency every single day. As you've explored the Leading by Design model throughout this book, you've seen how each quadrant—Clarity of Purpose, Setting Direction, Consistent Execution, Connection, Compliance, and Go Forward Development—provides a foundational pillar for effective leadership. This model isn't theoretical; it's a system for daily action and long-term impact.

But theory alone doesn't create change. To truly lead by design, you need to integrate this model into your daily, weekly, and quarterly leadership rhythms. This chapter is designed to help you operationalize the model—to give you a clear blueprint for how to lead intentionally every day, plan strategically for the long term, and measure success along the way.

Leadership isn't about perfection. It's about process. Let's explore how you can use the Leading by Design model to structure your leadership practice at every level: quarterly, weekly, daily, and when things go wrong.

At the Beginning of the Quarter: Planning for Success

Quarterly planning is the foundation of strategic leadership. The start of a new quarter presents the perfect opportunity to reset, refocus, and ensure your leadership is aligned with both personal and organizational objectives.

Clarity of Purpose: Reaffirm your leadership "why." Why are you leading this team? How does your leadership align with the organization's mission? Write it down and revisit it throughout the quarter. Do your people know their why and connection to the vision?

Setting Direction: Define specific, measurable goals for the quarter using the SMART framework. Align personal, team, and organizational objectives so everyone is moving in the same direction. How are you going to communicate?

Consistent Execution: Identify key projects and initiatives requiring focus. Block time for strategic work and leadership development. You get to set the priorities for yourself and the team. Get their involvement as well.

Connection: Plan relationship-building activities—team check-ins, mentorship pairings, and quarterly feedback sessions. Offsites.

Compliance: Review organizational policies and ensure alignment with leadership practices. Revisit accountability frameworks to maintain fairness and integrity. Are there any new risks at hand?

Go Forward Development: Identify growth opportunities for both yourself and your team. Assign mentors, plan learning opportunities, and build personal development plans for each team member.

Quarterly Reflection Questions:

Have I clearly defined what success looks like for this quarter?

How will I measure progress along the way?

Who on my team needs additional development or mentorship?

Sunday Nights: Preparing for the Week Ahead

A great week begins with clarity. Use the Leading by Design model to set the stage for a productive and purposeful week.

Clarity of Purpose: Revisit your leadership purpose and remind yourself why you lead. Anchor your weekly goals in that purpose. How will you inspire and keep the vision in front of your team?

Setting Direction: Outline the top priorities for the week. Ensure they align with quarterly goals and clearly define what success looks like. Communicate the priorities to your team.

Consistent Execution: Time-block your calendar for strategic work, meetings, and personal development. Identify your key focus areas for the week. Challenge your team to do the same.

Connection: Plan one-on-one meetings and team check-ins. Review any personal milestones or feedback conversations scheduled for the week.

Compliance: Confirm any necessary policy updates, performance evaluations, or process reviews are on track. What risks could arise?

Go Forward Development: Identify a learning opportunity for yourself and a growth moment for a team member. What can you celebrate as a team?

Sunday Night Questions:

What are my top priorities this week?

Where do I need to show up as a role model, teacher, or challenger?

Have I blocked time for what matters most?

Daily Leadership Practice: Leading with Intention

Consistent leadership happens in the daily moments. The Leading by Design model provides clarity on how you should show up every day.

Morning Reflection:

Identify your top three priorities for the day.

Review scheduled meetings and ensure they align with your leadership goals.

Throughout the Day:

Clarity of Purpose: Reinforce your purpose in conversations and decisions.

Setting Direction: Provide clear expectations during meetings and assignments. Adjust as the day and demands adjust. Communicate those adjustments.

Consistent Execution: Stick to your time blocks and minimize distractions. Use your power of saying "No." Reinforce for the team.

Connection: Engage in brief check-ins and mentorship moments. Celebrate right in the moments.

Compliance: Address issues of fairness, accountability, and policy alignment as they arise.

Go Forward Development: Create micro-learning moments through coaching and feedback. Challenge your team to be teaching one another.

Evening Reflection:

Did I stay aligned with my leadership purpose today?

Did the team make progress?

What adjustments are needed tomorrow?

End of the Week: Measuring Progress

The end of the week offers a powerful moment for reflection and refinement.

Clarity of Purpose: Reflect on whether your leadership stayed anchored to your core purpose. Did your team seemed aligned?

Setting Direction: Assess if the team made progress toward the week's goals. Was the prioritization helpful?

Consistent Execution: Review completed tasks and determine if time was effectively managed. What should e have said, "No" to?

Connection: Gather feedback from team interactions and check in on morale. What did we not celebrate and should have?

Compliance: Verify if all policies and standards were upheld consistently.

Go Forward Development: Identify growth moments from the week and plan for the next.

End of the Week Reflection Questions:

Did I lead with clarity and intention this week?

Where can I be more proactive next week?

Have I celebrated the team's wins and recognized individual contributions?

Using the Model When Things Go Wrong

Challenges and setbacks are inevitable. The Leading by Design model provides a framework for diagnosing issues and course-correcting.

Clarity of Purpose: Was the vision unclear? Did the team lack alignment on why their work matters?

Setting Direction: Were the goals ambiguous or poorly communicated?

Consistent Execution: Was there a breakdown in prioritization, time management, tools, systems, or delegation?

Connection: Were relationships strained? Did communication break down?

Compliance: Was there a failure to uphold standards or policies?

Go Forward Development: Were growth opportunities ignored or overlooked?

The Power of Applying Leading by Design

The Leading by Design model isn't a checklist—it's a way of leading intentionally, every single day. By using this model to plan, lead, and reflect, you create a leadership process that is repeatable, scalable, and transformative.

You don't have to be perfect. You don't need all the answers. What matters is that you commit to the process, show up with clarity, and keep striving for growth.

Leadership isn't something you do—it's who you become. Use this model as your guide, and you'll lead with purpose, clarity, and impact in every season of leadership.

Progress, Not Perfection

Here's the truth: you won't get it all right. And that's okay. Leadership isn't about being perfect—it's about being intentional. It's about showing up every day with a commitment to grow, improve, and lead with purpose.

The **Leading by Design Operating Model** isn't a destination; it's a roadmap. It's a tool you'll return to again and again as your leadership evolves. Each time you revisit it, you'll discover new opportunities to refine your approach and deepen your impact.

So, as you take your first steps, remember: leadership is a journey. Progress, not perfection, is the goal. One step at a time is how you'll build momentum, create change, and lead by design. The path ahead is yours to create—start walking.

Challenges on the Path to Leadership Excellence

Let's not sugarcoat it: leadership is hard. It's not just about hitting goals or managing teams—it's about making the tough calls, navigating uncertainty, and staying the course when the road gets rough. Leadership asks more of you than almost anything else. And yet, for those who embrace its challenges with intention and grit, the rewards are profound.

Here's the truth: If leadership feels easy, you're probably not doing it right. The best leaders don't shy away from the hard parts—they lean in. They wrestle with tough decisions, confront their blind spots, and learn to thrive in discomfort. They know that growth doesn't happen in a comfort zone.

Acknowledging the Struggles

Leadership isn't glamorous. It's late nights wrestling with decisions that have no clear answers. It's moments of self-doubt when you wonder if you're up to the task. It's balancing relentless demands while trying to stay true to your values and vision.

There will be times when you feel like you've failed—when a project tanks, when a team member leaves, or when you make a call that doesn't pan out. There will be days when the weight of responsibility feels crushing. But here's what separates great leaders from the rest: they don't let these moments define them. They see them as part of the process.

Staying Grounded During Setbacks

Setbacks are inevitable. What matters is how you respond. Do you let them derail you, or do you use them as fuel to move forward?

Practical Strategies to Stay Grounded:

- **Pause and Reflect:** When setbacks occur, take a moment to step back and process what happened. Ask yourself: What can I learn from this? What's the next best step?
- **Focus on the Bigger Picture:** Remember your purpose and long-term goals. A single setback doesn't define your leadership—it's just a chapter in a much larger story.
- **Lean on Your Values:** In moments of uncertainty, let your values guide you. They're the compass that keeps you steady when the path ahead is unclear.

The Power of Resilience and Adaptability

Resilience isn't about avoiding failure; it's about bouncing back stronger. And adaptability isn't about being reactive; it's about staying flexible and open to change. Together, these qualities are the backbone of leadership excellence.

Resilience:

When the going gets tough, resilient leaders don't crumble—they pivot. They find ways to recharge, refocus, and recommit. Resilience isn't about pretending everything's fine; it's about acknowledging the challenges and choosing to keep moving forward.

Adaptability:

The best leaders don't cling to rigid plans or outdated strategies—they adapt. They embrace uncertainty as an opportunity to innovate, learn, and grow. Adaptability isn't a weakness; it's a superpower in a world that's constantly changing.

Seeking Mentorship and Feedback

Here's a secret: no great leader does it alone. The best leaders surround themselves with mentors, peers, and teams who challenge, support, and guide them.

Mentorship:

A good mentor is more than a sounding board—they're a mirror that reflects both your strengths and your blind spots. Seek out mentors who've walked the path before you and can offer insights you haven't yet discovered. And remember: mentorship is a two-way street. Be open to both giving and receiving.

Feedback:

Feedback isn't criticism—it's a gift. It's how you grow, adapt, and refine your leadership. The key is to seek it actively, listen without defensiveness, and act on what you learn.

The Rewards of Intentional Leadership

Here's the thing about leadership: the challenges are real, but so are the rewards. When you lead with intention, you create impact. You inspire people, build teams that thrive, and leave organizations better than you found them.

Intentional leadership is hard, but it's worth it. It's worth it because of the people you empower, the cultures you shape, and the legacies you build. It's worth it because of the progress you make—not just as a leader, but as a human being.

Key Message

Challenges aren't roadblocks—they're stepping stones. They're the moments that test your resilience, sharpen your skills, and remind you why you chose to lead in the first place. Great leadership isn't about avoiding challenges—it's about embracing them, learning from them, and using them to grow.

The path isn't easy, but it's rewarding. And the best part? You don't have to walk it alone. Seek support, stay grounded, and never lose sight of the bigger picture. Because when you lead with intention, the impact you create makes every challenge worth it.

Leadership as an Ongoing Process

Here's the thing about leadership: it's never finished. There's no ribbon-cutting ceremony, no trophy, no "mission accomplished" banner. Leadership is a living, breathing process—one that evolves as you do. The moment you think you've mastered it is the moment you've stopped leading.

Great leaders understand that there's always more to learn, more to refine, more to give. They don't see leadership as a destination; they see it as a journey—one that requires constant reflection, growth, and curiosity. That's what makes leadership not just a role, but a craft.

The Continuous Guide

The **Leading by Design Operating Model** isn't a checklist you complete or a box you tick. It's a framework meant to grow with you. Each quadrant—Clarity of Purpose, Setting Direction, Consistent Execution, Connection, Compliance, and Go Forward Development—offers a lens through which to view your leadership. But those lenses aren't static.

As you face new challenges, lead new teams, or step into new roles, you'll find yourself revisiting these principles with fresh eyes. What "Connection" means for a small, close-knit team might look completely different when you're leading a larger, more dispersed group. What "Compliance" requires in a startup will shift as that same company grows into a complex organization.

That's the beauty of this model—it meets you where you are and grows with you as you evolve. It's not just a tool; it's a partner in your leadership journey.

Leadership is a Journey, Not a Destination

The best leaders embrace the idea that they're always a work in progress. They don't shy away from feedback, failure, or the discomfort of growth. Instead, they lean into it, knowing that every challenge is an opportunity to learn and every setback is a chance to improve.

Curiosity as a Superpower

Curiosity fuels great leadership. Leaders who stay curious—about their teams, their industries, and themselves—remain adaptable and innovative. They ask questions like:

- What's working, and what isn't?
- How can I better support my team?
- What skills do I need to develop next?

Curiosity doesn't just keep leaders sharp—it keeps them humble. It reminds them that no matter how much they know, there's always more to discover.

Embracing the Process

If there's one thing to take away from this book, it's this: leadership isn't something you do once. It's something you practice, refine, and commit to for as long as you lead. The **Leading by Design Operating Model** is your guide, but the work? That's up to you.

So keep showing up. Keep learning. Keep striving to make a difference—not just for yourself, but for your team, your organization, and the people whose lives you touch.

Because leadership, at its core, is an ongoing process. It's not about being perfect—it's about being present. It's about the journey, not the destination. And if you embrace that journey with commitment and curiosity, you'll find that the impact you make will far outlast your tenure.

Leadership doesn't end. It evolves. So should you.

Conclusion: The Call to Lead by Design

Leadership isn't reserved for the chosen few. It's not about titles, innate traits, or an elite set of skills possessed only by a select group. Leadership is a skill—a mindset—and like any skill, it can be learned, honed, and mastered.

If you've made it to this point, you already understand something many don't: leadership is a choice. It's a decision to show up with intention, to embrace the responsibility of guiding others, and to commit to growth—for yourself and those you lead. **The question isn't whether you're capable of leading; it's whether you're willing to make that choice every day.**

The **Leading by Design Operating Model** isn't just a framework. It's a philosophy for creating lasting impact. It's a way to lead with clarity, purpose, and accountability, while building the kind of trust, growth, and connection that transforms teams and organizations. It's about designing leadership—not leaving it to chance.

Putting It Into Action

Now it's time to step off the page and into the real world. Leadership doesn't happen in the abstract—it happens in the moments you choose to act. It happens in the one-on-one conversations where you listen with empathy, the meetings where you align your team around a shared purpose, and the hard decisions where you lean on your values to guide the way.

Take what you've learned here and make it your own. Share the model with your team and invite them on the journey. Use it to reflect on where you are and where you want to grow. But most importantly, put it into practice—not tomorrow, not next week, but today.

Because leadership isn't about perfection—it's about progress. It's not about knowing the right answers; it's about asking the right questions. It's not about being in control; it's about building trust, connection, and a legacy that lasts. **Its about YOUR process.**

HERE TO HELP

Here to Help: Partnering with Paratus Consulting

Leadership is a journey, but you don't have to walk it alone. At **Paratus Consulting LLC**, we specialize in helping organizations implement the **Leading by Design Operating Model** to create lasting impact. Whether you're looking to develop your leaders, build high-performing teams, or align your organization around a common vision, we're here to guide you every step of the way.

Our Services

At Paratus Consulting, we offer a suite of services designed to meet the unique needs of your organization and ensure leadership excellence:

- **Leadership Development Workshops:** Engage your leaders in hands-on, practical workshops designed to teach and apply the Leading by Design principles.
- **Executive Coaching:** Work one-on-one with experienced coaches to refine leadership skills, set strategic goals, and overcome challenges.
- **Team Alignment Sessions:** Bring your teams together to build trust, clarify objectives, and foster a culture of collaboration and accountability.
- **Custom Leadership Frameworks:** Tailor the Leading by Design model to fit your organization's specific goals, challenges, and culture.

- **Strategic Planning Facilitation:** Align leadership strategies with organizational objectives to drive long-term success.
- **Succession Planning and Development:** Prepare your next generation of leaders with actionable plans for growth and readiness.

We understand that every organization is unique, which is why our solutions are customized to your team's needs, goals, and values.

Why Partner with Paratus Consulting?

Our approach goes beyond theory. We focus on practical, actionable solutions that create measurable results. With decades of experience in leadership development, strategic planning, and team building, we've worked with organizations across industries to empower leaders and transform teams.

When you partner with us, you're not just adopting a framework—you're gaining a dedicated team committed to your success. Our vision is to help you create a culture where leadership thrives, trust flourishes, and goals are achieved with clarity and purpose.

About the Author

Robert Barber is a seasoned leadership trainer, consultant, and executive coach with over 26 years of experience across executive HR, serial entrepreneurship, engineering, sales, and marketing. He has dedicated his career to helping leaders and organizations engineer high performance in leadership development, organizational strategy, and human capital management.

As the best-selling author of **CEO For Life**, Robert is known for his innovative training programs, masterminds, and his ability to turn complex leadership concepts into practical, actionable strategies. He is the founder and lead coach of **Paratus Consulting**, where he focuses on high-performance leadership training and HR strategy for organizations looking to elevate their impact.

Before launching Paratus Consulting, Robert held key leadership roles, including serving as an **Operating Principal at a multimillion-dollar luxury residential and commercial investment firm** and as the **Executive Leader of HR at a Fortune 150 company**. His unique combination of technical expertise, business acumen, and people-first leadership has earned him a reputation as a transformative coach and consultant.

Robert holds a **Bachelor of Science in Electrical Engineering** and an **MBA**, but he credits much of his leadership philosophy to his early career as a **Walt Disney World Jungle Cruise Captain**, where he learned the value of storytelling, engagement, and creating unforgettable experiences.

Robert's vision is simple: to help leaders unlock their potential, build thriving teams, and create lasting impact. Through his work at Paratus Consulting and his authorship of the **Leading by Design Operating Model**, he continues to empower leaders to approach their roles with clarity, purpose, and intention.

Let's Build Together

Leadership by design is more than a concept—it's a transformative approach to creating impact, engagement, and growth. If you're ready to take the next step, we'd be honored to partner with you.

Visit us at Paratus Consulting LLC to learn more about our services, explore how we can support your leadership journey, and connect with our team. Together, let's design a leadership model that drives success for your organization and creates a lasting legacy.

Printed in Dunstable, United Kingdom

65039123R00127